D0500377

LONE STAR
AMERICA

LONE STAR AMERICA

AMERICA

HOW TEXAS CAN
SAVE OUR COUNTRY

MARK DAVIS

RADIO TALK SHOW HOST

REGNERY
PUBLISHING

A Salem Communications Company

Cataloging-in-Publication data on file with the Library of Congress

ISBN 978-1-62157-225-1

Published in the United States by
Regnery Publishing
A Salem Communications Company
300 New Jersey Avenue NW
Washington, DC 20001
www.Regnery.com

Manufactured in the United States of America

10 9 8 7 6 5 4 3 2 1

Books are available in quantity for promotional or premium use. For information on discounts and terms, please visit our website: www.Regnery.com.

Distributed to the trade by
Perseus Distribution
250 West 57th Street
New York, NY 10107

To my wonderful children, Regina and Ethan, and most of all to Lisa, my cherished wife at the center of my Texas life

CONTENTS

Part VI: Red, Blue, and Purple: Different States, Different Fates

Part VII: Lone Star Luminaries

Part VIII: Conclusion

FOREWORD
By Sean Hannity

Texas is the home of freedom and independence, and it's a state that strongly believes in the Constitution.

Mark Davis and I have been good friends for many years, and it is an honor to know a man of such great character who has been fighting endlessly for his state of Texas, as well as the rest of the country. It's a pleasure to write this foreword because like Mark, I have dedicated my life to seeing America succeed.

Texas is an extraordinary success story. It's a state full of jobs, opportunity, and prosperity, and it should be a model for our entire country. Texans have the sense to elect leaders like Rick Perry and Ted Cruz, who know what it takes to prosper. Look at the results: Texas has no state income tax and is projected to have an $8 billion surplus in 2015.

Meanwhile, places like my home state of New York are always looking to pick your pocket. The Empire State helps itself to nearly 10 percent of my income, and I pay the highest property taxes in the country. When Governor Andrew Cuomo declared that conservatives have no place in New York, I realized he may be right. That's why I'm looking to leave and move to a prosperous state like Texas.

Of all the dismal statistics that define Barack Obama's economy, none is more discouraging than the record number of people on government assistance. Forty-seven million Americans receive food stamps, a number that has almost doubled since Obama became president. Over forty-six million Americans live in poverty. In 2013 the percentage of the population participating in the labor force hit its lowest level in thirty-five years. But in the midst of America's seemingly endless economic winter, we keep hearing about a place where things are different—a place where big government hasn't crushed the spirit of freedom and enterprise that leads to prosperity. That place is Texas, and Mark Davis is here to tell you that everything you've heard is true.

You may ask yourself, "Is Texas the last, best hope for an America that's headed toward a cliff?"

As Marks shows, it may not be the *last* hope, but it's the *best* hope. The United States won't turn into Greece in the next year, but strong, unapologetically conservative leadership can help every state chart a course toward more jobs, more liberty, and happier people. That's a lesson the whole nation should learn as it goes to the polls in 2014, 2016, and beyond.

Texans have their problems like everyone else, of course, but whether it's energy policy or taxes and spending, education or the environment, they usually get it right. And when it comes to the fundamentals, Texas proves that the values of faith, family, and freedom aren't so old-fashioned after all.

The American Dream isn't dead, but it seems to have developed a Texas accent. Mark Davis is ready to show you around the place where America still works. Do yourself a favor and start turning these pages.

INTRODUCTION

One is either a native Texan or not. I am, by a slim margin.

Uncle Sam stationed my father at Randolph Air Force Base in San Antonio in 1956. My birth the following year conferred Native Texan status, which I proudly brandished as soon as I learned how to brandish things.

It mattered not one bit that Mom and Dad were packing to leave barely a year later, whisking me off for a decidedly un-Texas childhood:

- Suburban Virginia, while Dad worked at the Pentagon;
- London, while Dad worked with the military attaché at the U.S. embassy;
- Suburban Maryland, as Dad returned to the Pentagon.

Not exactly a youth spent on horseback lassoing cattle among oil derricks. But after years of young adulthood wrangling radio jobs across the South, capped with a return to Washington to live and work inside the Beltway as a grownup, fate—or as I prefer to think of it, benevolent Providence—brought me back to Texas twenty years ago. My return completed a magnificent circle that has allowed me to raise a family here, plant inextractable roots here, climb a ladder of professional blessings here, and now to write a book about Texas and why it is of such value to a troubled America.

Texas is a sure-fire conversation starter. Its residents and supporters are passionate and proud, its detractors edgy and snarky. The debate over its triumphs and flaws mirrors the national conversation about how to cure America's many ills.

A book about Texas by a lifelong Texan would be valuable enough. It would be filled with appreciation born of an uninterrupted lifetime of Lone Star values, experiences, anecdotes, and lessons. But the deepest appreciation for Texas is often found in people who are from somewhere else, or who were once here and had to move away. Or who were born here, grew up somewhere else, and were blessed to return.

A popular Texas bumper sticker boasts, "I wasn't born here, but I got here as fast as I could." Mine would say, "I *was* born here but raised elsewhere. Thank God I got to come back." Too wordy for a bumper sticker, I know. In fact, it takes a whole book to identify properly the virtues of Texas and why they are urgently needed by a nation being dragged toward massive, predatory government and away from traditional values.

There have been plenty of books and articles about Texas, some worshipful, some appreciative, some critical, some insulting.

Writers look at Texas and what it represents through different lenses. Historians and academics have taken up the subject of Texas; I am neither. I am a radio guy and a writer whose head is filled with experiences and conversations from inside and outside my state. The points I make are sometimes connected to hard data or the historical record, but just as often they are the product of what I've done and the people I've met.

In thirty-five years of broadcasting and writing in Texas and elsewhere, I've learned from slinging opinions around as history unfolds and trading views with talk show callers and guests. The last twenty years of that adventure have been spent right here in the state of my birth. Blessed with a magnificent Texas wife and the family that comes with her, with one child raised here and the other born here, I have personally enjoyed the glories of the modern Texas experience—the one that has people tripping over each other to move here, as formerly booming states bleed population under stagnant, oppressive governance.

For Texans, I hope this is a handy guide to what you already know and love but surely enjoy hearing again, spiced with some stories you have not heard.

For curious non-Texans, I hope it explains what all the fuss is about.

And for critical non-Texans, consider it a conversation starter.

How can a state have so many fans and so many detractors? Who is right? Why is Texas in the news all the time? Might we get another president from Texas—the rock star Ted Cruz or a seasoned, wiser Rick Perry?

As we slog our way through the second term of Barack Obama, two samples of public opinion stand out: while whopping majorities of Americans believe the nation is heading in the wrong direction, most Texans say their state is on the right track.[1] Of course, people's perception of the "right track" is largely a product of their personal situation. There are people who believe that expansionist, collectivist government and profligate spending are steps in the right direction. They do not run Texas. As a result, the state has become a glowing example of how to survive, and even thrive, as Washington bends leftward.

Your state may be red, blue, or purple. Every state would benefit from low taxes, sensible regulation, productive energy policies, secure property rights, and fidelity to the Constitution.

And dare we dream? Maybe if enough states follow Texas, we will elevate national leaders with the same instincts. There's plenty to complain about these days, but we just might fix this country yet.

PART I

THE
TEXAS
MYSTIQUE

CHAPTER ONE

THE STATE THAT WORKS

The election of 2012 was a brutal disappointment for American conservatives. Republicans were left reeling from the loss of a presidential race that had seemed so winnable. Worse still, this wasn't just any election—it was the reset button for Barack Obama, who offered the nation another heaping helping of policies that sped past mainstream liberalism toward statism and even socialism.

In Texas, we knew our electors would not be tallied in the Obama column. But on that dark night of November 6, 2012, we saw several "swing" states swing the other way: Ohio, Florida, Pennsylvania, Michigan, Virginia, Wisconsin, Iowa, New Mexico—there were more, but those states were particularly bitter losses.

They all had Republican governors.

Voters in those states, who had opted, often quite recently, for conservative leadership, decided in the 2012 presidential election that they wanted something vastly different.

In Texas, this drove us nuts.

Our passion for close-to-home government runs so deep that our state capital scarcely runs our schools. We have over a thousand "independent school districts" (ISDs), a system that reflects our determination that decisions be made where we live, not by distant bureaucrats. In most matters, we want our state governed by people we elect right here, not by Washington.

The ascendancy of President Obama has compelled many states to craft responses to an administration that seeks to impose its will at the federal level. Texas is not the only state that has pushed back, but our resistance garnered extra attention because of our size and our governor.

When Rick Perry was sworn in as governor of Texas, Bill Clinton was in his last days in the White House. Lieutenant Governor Perry filled the vacancy in the governor's office left by George W. Bush, who was preparing for his inauguration as president the following month. The Perry years have thus encompassed the last month of Clinton, eight years of President Bush, and both elections of Barack Obama. When Perry leaves office in January 2015, the race to determine Obama's successor will be well under way.

Some of that speculation will involve Perry, to the befuddlement of many elites. How, they wonder, can someone known only for a debate-stage brain cramp have credibility in the very next election? It is simple. While Perry may have vapor-locked in November 2011 on the third agency he would eliminate as president, even critics will admit he never grew foggy about the principle that has guided his governorship and would define him as a national leader: keeping the federal government out of the states' business.

His devotion to this concept led him in the summer of 2011 to acknowledge New York's right to recognize same-sex marriage even though he disagreed with it. The Left pounced on this statement as an inconsistency, and more than a few conservatives raised an eyebrow, wondering if Perry had revealed a soft spot in his social conservatism.

The resulting fire from both sides forced Perry into the kind of detailed postscript that is treacherous on the campaign trail. Yes, he favored a constitutional amendment defining marriage as the union of one man and one woman. But in the absence of such an amendment, the Constitution is silent on the issue, and its Tenth Amendment requires that the matter be left to the states and to the people. It's disappointing, if not surprising, that this response satisfied very few people. His reasoning isn't tough to follow: the Constitution says what it says, and that's what should rule the day. In an era when leaders declare everything they support to be constitutional and everything they oppose to be unconstitutional, Perry offered a thoughtful and modest judgment about the Constitution. And that, of course, got him in trouble.

Memories of that dustup have largely faded, but Perry remains front and center on the national stage, even though he is a short-timer in public office. His successor will be chosen in November 2014, and he will leave office two months later. But he seems to be everywhere, a sought-after voice for states' rights and a champion of Texas's record of fending off the ill effects of Obama's policies.

In the fall of 2013, Perry helped launch Americans for Economic Freedom, a group with a deliciously broad title offering yet another platform for Perry to promote his brand of conservatism. There is speculation, naturally, that AEF is a springboard, or at least a trial balloon, for another presidential run. With the Iowa caucuses more than two years away, he has said nothing about that, but the organization's thirty-second ad did little to douse the speculation: "It isn't hard to see what's right in front of you," his voice-over begins, amid scenes of urban blight. "Washington needs to change. But the president keeps playing politics." An image of a finger-wagging Obama gives way to a smiling Perry in front of a sun-splashed Texas capitol. "When I look around this country, there's another story. Conservative governors are reforming taxes and regulations, helping small businesses grow, cutting and balancing budgets." Then the sell: "Conservative leadership is putting people back to work …" The image: Perry chatting with workers happy to enjoy his company and his policies. Then a dad reaching for his daughter's hand: "… and families are building their futures. We need more of that and less of Washington."

Perry closes with an invitation to join Americans for Economic Freedom, but his message is broader. The remedy for two terms of Barack Obama—indeed, the best defense against liberal mischief from any source—is devotion to pro-business policies and a pro-family ethic.

Perry's ad can be a debate starter, and opposing voices will rush in to criticize his policies as harmful to the poor, minorities, women, whomever. But can the Left point to any state whose policies are yielding Texas-type results? The fear that California might one day slide into the ocean has been replaced by the more plausible concern that it will slide into unprecedented economic ruin.

In a nation with a twice-elected Democratic president and a Democratic Senate majority that has held power for most of this young century, Republican governors nevertheless outnumbered Democrats in 2013 by a margin of twenty-nine to twenty-one. None of them has had the political longevity or impact of Perry. And before him came George W. Bush. It's clear that leading America's second-most-populous state in a conservative direction can garner a lot of attention. It took Bush to the presidency (with a little help from his family name), and it has taken Perry to national conservative prominence, perhaps with further historic chapters in store. The common thread that unites these two personal and political success stories is their ability to boost the Republican brand in a state filled with minorities, union workers, and other traditionally Democratic constituencies. Texas, of course, spent most of its history under uninterrupted Democratic rule. Other than Perry and Bush, there have been only three Republican governors since the state was admitted to the Union in 1845. Yet today, the clock is ticking toward the twentieth anniversary of Republican domination in Texas.

Ever since Bush shocked Ann Richards by beating her in the 1994 governor's race, Texas has been a laboratory for conservative government: low taxes, reduced regulation, sensible spending, and faith-based social policies. The impressive results are there for anyone willing to examine them honestly. The Left sidesteps Texas's inconvenient success by painting the state as a benighted backwater filled with undereducated kids, suffering immigrants, low-wage jobs, and yahoos who just can't wait to beat you over the head with a Bible. That picture breaks down as soon as someone visits here, or moves here, or does a little research to see why people are rushing here to start businesses, raise families, and put down roots.

When colleagues from other states ask me why I insist I will never leave Texas, they make comparisons based on topography and attractions. Our beaches are not Florida's. Our mountains are not Colorado's. We do not have Disney World or Las Vegas casinos.

But here's what we do have—Texans. Lots of them, full of energy and ambition. I can visit either ocean or any mountain or any theme park any time I wish. But for a place to live, to work, to raise a family, give me Texas.

That's not to say there aren't wonderful places all across the American map where happiness and prosperity abound. But there is something singular about the Texas way of governing and living that merits attention. After my Texas birth, Maryland upbringing, and early professional stops in West Virginia, Florida, and Tennessee, I noticed that people just would not shut up about Texas. I wondered why. Now I know.

There is a cohesiveness here that defies description, a shared identity that is spoken of constantly, from political campaigns to TV commercials. Upon my return in 1994, I noticed that national brands customized their advertising just for this. One familiar jingle was "Ford is the best in Texas." I never remembered ads in Memphis telling me Chevy was tops in Tennessee. Sure, part of that is simple volume. We have twenty-six million people. That's a lot of potential customers. But Illinois, Pennsylvania, and Ohio are top-ten population states, and I'm betting they generally get the same ads everyone else gets.

Whether you're pitching trucks or candidates, it's wise to call on Texans by name. Our political ads speak often of "Texas values," and both Republicans and Democrats use the phrase.

Republicans couch those values in conservative terms, while our feisty Democrats assert that "Texas values" include spending more tax dollars on schools and giving everyone health insurance. Candidates of both parties try to portray themselves as embodying all that is characteristically Texan: courage, independence, resilience.

Despite this shared vocabulary, though, political boundaries in Texas are sharpening. For a long time, you could find lots of Texas Republicans with a populist streak and moderate views. And some of our Democrats have been more conservative than some New England Republicans. Maybe it's the ascendancy of Barack Obama, or the resulting rise of the Tea Party. Maybe it's the instant star status enjoyed by freshman Senator Ted Cruz. Whatever the catalyst, Texas Republicans are leaning farther to the right while our Democrats tack left. This polarization isn't surprising. Obama lost Texas by 12 points in 2008, and 16 in 2012, but a statewide Democratic party thirsting for a return to influence has kept its wagon hitched to this administration, maintaining its fealty to Obamacare, big spending, and, more vocally lately, abortion rights. Meanwhile, Texas Republicans launched Cruz to national prominence while rejecting his primary rival, Lieutenant Governor David Dewhurst, a respected longtime leader who co-piloted the state with Rick Perry to prosperity in tough times. So what happened? Cruz projected the persona of a fighter, while Dewhurst's attributes—legislative prowess and the ability to make deals in the deliberative march toward conservative goals—made him look like Mr. Establishment. After four years of gnashing their teeth in the darkness of the Obama regime, Texas Republicans preferred long downfield passes to three yards and a cloud of dust.

The same sentiments swayed the 2012 races all the way down the ballot. Tea Party candidates ousted longtime state lawmakers who had been conservative enough just a few years earlier. As the 2014 primary season drew near, some Texas members of Congress drew primary opponents with a Cruz flavor seeking to raise the bar for conservative credibility. The day after Mitt Romney lost the presidency, my talk show was inundated with calls from listeners instantly yearning for the 2016 White House battle—not just because it will bring the Obama years to a welcome end, but because it will be an opportunity to look for a nominee without the flaws of Romney or John McCain, for whom Texas Republicans had to settle in 2008 and 2012 because our primary came so late in the season.

The success of Texas stands out all the more starkly against the national misery of the Obama years. Ideologues of the Left do their best to deny it or explain it away, but other Americans are noticing our prosperity and wondering how they can share it. Texans aren't the only ones who are hungry for leadership in Washington that will move the entire nation along the path Texas has followed.

CHAPTER TWO

WHY EVERYONE SHOULD REMEMBER THE ALAMO

T exas politics start with Texas history. Every state has had its own path to the Union, but Texas's story sets it apart, inspiring and informing the Texans of today and shaping the state's character.

At the heart of Texas history is the battle cry "Remember the Alamo!" When I first learned how the Battle of the Alamo turned out, I wondered why everyone was so eager to remember it. It was in junior high school American history, 1,200 miles from Texas in Prince George's County, Maryland, that I first understood why the Alamo was worth remembering. The importance of the battle comes from the sacrifice offered there and in the surprising twist of history that followed it.

On March 6, 1836, after two weeks of fending off the Mexican armies of General Antonio López de Santa Anna, the last of roughly two hundred Alamo defenders died. The battlefield did not fall immediately silent. Various historians describe a rampage of wanton shooting even after the last Texian* defender was killed. Yet only a few weeks after this stinging defeat, Texas won its independence. How was that possible?

That's where the mystique of the Alamo lies—a mystique I didn't understand until I returned to Texas as an adult and an experience at a political fundraiser, of all places, branded it on my heart forever. With a few years of hosting Texas talk shows under my belt, I received a request to serve as master of ceremonies for Congressman Joe Barton's annual "Happy Birthday, Texas" fundraiser. Elected in 1984, Barton represents a district that stretches southward from the Dallas–Fort Worth suburbs halfway to Houston. The "birthday" referred to is March 2, Texas Independence Day.

While William Barret Travis, the twenty-six-year-old lieutenant colonel in command of the Texians at the Alamo, waited with his men for the Mexican attack and certain death, delegates gathered 150 miles to the east in Washington-on-the-Brazos and issued the declaration of independence that marked the birth of the Republic of Texas. On February 24, the second day of the siege, Travis had written a letter, to be published as widely as possible, calling for reinforcements. I first heard Travis's letter, which is familiar to schoolchildren all over Texas, when Congressman Barton read it that day at his fundraiser. It is the soul of patriotism, and it never gets old:

---

* "Texians" were residents of Texas when it was under Mexican control from 1821 until independence was won, in 1836. The term remained in use for another decade when Texas was an independent republic. When Texas was admitted to the Union as the twenty-eighth state, in 1845, the middle syllable began to disappear and the term "Texan" became the norm.

To the People of Texas & All Americans in the World:

Fellow citizens & compatriots—I am besieged, by a thousand or more of the Mexicans under Santa Anna—I have sustained a continual Bombardment & cannonade for 24 hours & have not lost a man. The enemy has demanded a surrender at discretion, otherwise, the garrison are to be put to the sword, if the fort is taken—I have answered the demand with a cannon shot, & our flag still waves proudly from the walls. *I shall never surrender or retreat.* Then, I call on you in the name of Liberty, of patriotism & everything dear to the American character, to come to our aid, with all dispatch—The enemy is receiving reinforcements daily & will no doubt increase to three or four thousand in four or five days. If this call is neglected, I am determined to sustain myself as long as possible & die like a soldier who never forgets what is due to his own honor & that of his country—*Victory or Death.*

—William Barret Travis

Lt. Col. comdt

P.S. The Lord is on our side—When the enemy appeared in sight we had not three bushels of corn— We have since found in deserted houses 80 or 90 bushels & got into the walls 20 or 30 head of Beeves.

Travis

Travis never got sufficient reinforcements, of course, but a few weeks later, the cry of "Remember the Alamo!" was on the lips of a thousand soldiers under the command of General Sam Houston as they overwhelmed Santa Anna's forces at the Battle of San Jacinto.

The Alamo, San Jacinto, the Texians' victory over Mexico, and the eventual admission of Texas to the Union in 1845 are central, quite literally, to the story of America's expansion across the continent. Before the Texas Revolution, the map of Mexico extended across what is now New Mexico, Arizona, and Southern California. The addition of those formerly Mexican territories fortified the concept of manifest destiny. Continued Mexican rule in Texas would have been a massive obstacle to the expansion of the United States west of the Mississippi.

Joe Barton and plenty of other Texas leaders are fond of reminding all who will listen of the way the dominoes fell: the Alamo led to San Jacinto, which led to the Republic of Texas, which led to statehood for Texas. Statehood for California came a scant five years later, along with the establishment of the New Mexico Territory. Arizona was formed from that stretch of land, and the last pieces of the map of the continental United States were in place.

Texans are proud of our decade as an independent nation. And if there's anything we enjoy doing these days, it is remarking where we would rank if we were independent again.

This has nothing to do with the fringe notion of secession, which arises in some corners whenever Washington's overreach grows particularly noxious—which is fairly often of late.

It is merely an appreciation of what we have achieved. According to Alberto Riva, writing in the *International Business Times*, if Texas were an independent country, it would be the fourteenth-biggest economy in the world, outpacing South Korea and the

Netherlands. Its $1.2 trillion gross domestic product would place it just behind Spain and, ironically enough, just ahead of Mexico.[1]

The story of Texas's economic power provides many lessons to a United States in need of an economic upswing. It is a story of energy, smart business practices, and wise self-governance. The historical roots of those successes go back to the Alamo, a building I did not in fact visit until after I had heard Joe Barton read Travis's letter.

The landscape on which the Alamo stands has changed, to say the least, in the nearly two centuries since the famous siege. Though the remaining structure is kept as a shrine, pilgrims face an abrupt transition from solemn history to tourist glitz as they step out onto Alamo Plaza with its hotspots like Ripley's Haunted Adventure and Tomb Rider 3-D. But no amount of commercialization can diminish the power of a visit to the Alamo, especially with Travis's words ringing in your mind. No photography or use of cell phones is allowed inside its sacred walls. Men are required to remove their hats, and a sign at the entrance enjoins:

Be silent, friend, here heroes died to blaze a trail for other men.

PART II

WIDE OPEN
FOR BUSINESS

CHAPTER THREE

THE TEXAS ECONOMY: MIRACLE OR MYTH?

T exas is getting lots of attention these days because of its vibrant economy. But if we're going to understand that economic vibrancy, where do we begin? Taxes? Spending? Regulation? Each deserves its own spotlight. Let's start with a column that one of conservatism's favorite villains, the Princeton economics professor Paul Krugman, wrote for the *New York Times* in August 2011.

Rick Perry had just announced his presidential run, sending a ripple of adrenaline through analysts on the Left. Outwardly, liberals smile broadly when a true conservative throws his hat into the ring. Perhaps they think a conservative opponent is easy to beat. Who knows if they're right? The GOP has not had a truly Reaganesque nominee since Reagan. But I have always believed that, deep down, thoughtful liberals worry about the ascendancy of a consistent, muscular conservative. Progressives can find common ground with a John McCain or a Mitt Romney, but an unwavering agenda of low taxes, reduced spending, and increased liberty is an existential threat. The Reagan presidency made "liberal" such a toxic label that they came up with "progressive" as a less damaging alternative.

So as Perry set off on the campaign trail, Krugman embarked on his own campaign to discredit the state that gave Perry instant national credibility. The "Texas miracle is a myth, and more broadly ... Texan experience offers no useful lessons on how to restore national full employment," Krugman insisted.[1] (That's an interesting placement of the bar. Is anyone talking about "full employment" these days? Deep into the second Obama term, it feels like a distant dream.)

In October 2008, at the worst point of the recession, the U.S. unemployment rate hit 10 percent. That same month, the Texas rate was 8.1 percent. It never went higher than 8.2.[2] So how does Krugman explain the state that best withstood the economic crash of 2008 and the subsequent years of lethargy? "Widespread misunderstanding of the economic effects of population growth." That misunderstanding must be widespread indeed, since millions have moved to Texas in search of opportunity their states simply cannot provide.

The Krugman theory is that "population growth translates into above-average job growth through a couple of channels. Many of the people moving to Texas—retirees in search of warm winters, middle-class Mexicans in search of a safer life—bring purchasing power that leads to greater local employment. At the same time, the rapid growth in the Texas work force keeps wages low ... and these low wages give corporations an incentive to move production to the Lone Star State."

What part of this is bad, exactly?

If there is a wage-suppressing effect in Texas, it is offset by the cost-of-living-suppressing effect, which is a magnet for countless families escaping the "higher wages" of states with collapsing economies. But Krugman's basic point—that Texas's economic growth is some undeserved function of population growth—fails to explain why the population is growing in the first place.

People are flocking to Texas to find what they are not finding in California, New York, and other states I could pick on: the opportunity to work and earn a prosperous, stable livelihood. The set of prospects that we poetically call the "American Dream" are darkened in much of America—mainly the states that share Krugman's politics.

He seems particularly enamored of Massachusetts and New York, with their stagnant populations and hit-or-miss economies. There is nothing more enlightening than seeing New Yorkers or Bostonians or people from other crushingly expensive areas discover how far their dollars could stretch in Dallas or Houston or San Antonio (to say nothing of our smaller towns, which are even more affordable). Teachers, cops, and private-sector workers do indeed enjoy higher salaries in many other states. But those extra dollars are wiped out by the higher costs of housing, food, healthcare, utilities, and most other things as well.

One of the best instant rebuttals of the Krugman column came from Kevin Williamson at National Review Online:

> In Houston, the median household income is 39 percent of the cost of a typical house. In Brooklyn, the median household income is 8 percent of the cost of

the median home, and in Boston it's only 14 percent. When it comes to homeownership, $1 in earnings in Houston is worth a lot more than $1 in Brooklyn or Boston. But even that doesn't really tell the story, because the typical house in Houston doesn't look much like the typical house in Brooklyn: Some 64 percent of the homes in Houston are single-family units, i.e., houses. In Brooklyn, 85 percent are multi-family units, i.e. apartments and condos.[3]

Most critics of Texas commit these same errors of phony equivalency. And federal statistics help them. National poverty rates are set without regard for a state's cost of living. There are plenty of Texas families living slightly below the national poverty line who are doing far better than families just above the poverty line in high-cost states.

Yes, wages in Texas are consistently lower than in New York or California—and people are flocking here to accept those wages because they are attracted to jobs that are more secure and buy more house, more food, more energy, and, yes, more healthcare than they ever afforded back home.

Texas's success is kryptonite to Krugman. "[A] state offering cheap labor and, less important, weak regulation can attract jobs from other states," he writes. "I believe that the appropriate response to this insight is 'Well, duh.' The point is that arguing from this experience that depressing wages and dismantling regulation in America as a whole would create more jobs—which is, whatever Mr. Perry may say, what Perrynomics amounts to in practice—involves a fallacy of composition: every state can't lure jobs away from every other state."

This is an Ivy League professor? A Nobel laureate? *Of course* every state cannot lure jobs away from every other state. But if the influx of people to Texas stopped tomorrow, the state's low taxes, sensible regulation, and pro-business philosophy would continue to fuel a strong economy that would keep Texans happy. And happiness is a precious commodity. "The pursuit of happiness" merited mention in the Declaration of Independence because it sums up what mankind seeks—the opportunity to live a fulfilled, productive life in a pleasing environment. That's why people move to Texas, to the chagrin of the sage of Princeton.

Krugman's vexation clouds his logic. He concludes his column, "In fact, at a national level lower wages would almost certainly lead to fewer jobs—because they would leave working Americans even less able to cope with the overhang of debt left behind by the housing bubble, an overhang that is at the heart of our economic problem."

Wow.

Come to Texas, Paul. Look around. What you would see is a state full of people who may not make the wages of your fellow Northeasterners but who actually have more left over after their expenses are met. A lower cost of living enhances the ability to cope with debt.

Shop for a place to live in Texas for $150,000. Then go house-hunting at that same price point in the states filled with enlightened leaders who tax and spend at Krugman-approved levels. The shocking difference should be an eye-opener to anyone honestly trying to compare the Texas economy and standard of living with those of other states. It should be, but it often is not. The benefits of the Texas way are on display for all to see, but the state still draws fire from those intimidated by its lessons.

CHAPTER FOUR

BAILOUT-FREE ZONE: THE VALUE OF FAILURE

Speaking well of failure may offend the sensibilities of an era that seeks to mitigate, redefine, or eliminate it. But for a growing child, a small business, or a megabank, failure can be instructive. It delivers the message that something has not been done properly. In the absence of that message, children grow up untrained, and businesses plow forward unmotivated to make wise decisions. How do we learn what to do if we don't occasionally learn what not to do? If success is unearned and failure never allowed to bite, you get a weak and pampered kid or a reckless business.

Fear of failure is one thing. Refusing to let it occur is quite another. When we go weak-kneed at the prospect of a failing manufacturer or a failing bank, we show we are unwilling to allow market forces to impart their vital lessons.

Even though a Texan president, George W. Bush, signed the Troubled Asset Relief Program (TARP) into law in October 2008, the Texas ethic has been to allow markets to bestow the blessings of success or to teach the lessons of failure, letting the chips fall where they may. Many a successful Texas business is a reboot of a venture that failed before—sometimes repeatedly, sometimes spectacularly. The common thread in such stories is resilience, the willingness to learn from mistakes and make a better product, deliver a better service, formulate a better business plan.

If we had lived by this ethic during the subprime mortgage crisis, we would have learned lessons that would be paying dividends today. The economy constricted in 2008, but we had been sowing the seeds of the crisis for more than a decade. Analysts identify different catalysts for the economic disaster, but there is no denying that a massive number of mortgages issued to people who had no hope of paying them off were at the heart of the problem, and all those "subprime" loans were the result of an idea that is the antithesis of Texas-style independence and personal responsibility: the dangerous notion that home ownership is a right.

Bill Clinton's secretary of housing and urban development, Henry Cisneros, enshrined this view in a 1995 report, *The National Homeownership Strategy: Partners in the American Dream*, which amounted to a wish list for bureaucrats, lenders, housing executives, and activists driven to change the template for home ownership.[1]

Consider a conversation that has occurred countless times through the years:

"I don't want to go to school."

"You have to go to school."

"Why?"

"So you can graduate and get a good job."

"Why?"

"So you can afford a nice house."

This is powerful stuff when you're nine. You imagine life in some dank hovel because you didn't show up for a math test decades earlier. But the message was clear: a house was something you acquired with your own money, which you earned by honest labors. It was not a right. No one was going to give it to you, not even because of your race or station in life.

Cisneros, who was the mayor of San Antonio before joining the Clinton administration, is a Texan of considerable accomplishment, but he was never a champion of self-sufficiency. Home ownership, the dream of most Americans, had always depended on the ability to pay for it. Redefining it as a right turned out to be a bad idea.

Oil, real estate, cotton, cattle, lumber, banking—these Texas industries have all seen booms and busts. When times are lean, the Texas spirit is to grit your teeth and ride it out.

Economic hardship has actually created a multitude of opportunities, as we saw in the early 1980s.

As the nation emerged from the economic misery of the Carter years, Texas found itself out of step with the rest of the country. The oil that had turbocharged the Texas economy suddenly turned around and delivered a sucker punch. A global recession suppressed demand as overproduction depressed prices. Oil woes led to real estate woes, leading to banking crises. Those banks learned a lesson in an era before anyone talked about "too big to fail." They learned that some failures are due to bad decisions, others to dumb luck. Eventually the insolvencies of the 1980s gave way to the recoveries of the 1990s, and Texas banks emerged so robust that they withstood the 2007–2009 recession. Hard times strengthen people, banks, businesses, and states.

The freedom to succeed presupposes the freedom to fail. President George W. Bush differed from my hard line on this, but nevertheless I appreciated him and his presidency. I expressed that appreciation on the air enough to land an unforgettable invitation as his presidency ticked down its final days.

On January 14, 2009, the president invited a gaggle of radio talk show hosts to the Oval Office to reflect on his years of service and our years of talking about it. I was honored to join my colleagues Mike Gallagher, Mark Levin, Michael Medved, Hugh Hewitt, Neal Boortz, and others to hear the president's personal thoughts as his era wound to a close. No questions were off-limits, but there is an etiquette for such occasions. None of us was going to start an argument with Mr. Bush while we sat in what was, for a few more days, his house.

When the subject of TARP and bailouts arose, however, I had to ask him why he chose a course so contrary to Texas wisdom. He recalled conversations with Treasury Secretary Henry Paulson, who assured him that the financial system was on the brink of collapse, a catastrophe that could be averted only by pouring hundreds of billions of taxpayer dollars into it.

The question I would have liked to ask but didn't was, "Why did you have to accept that spin? Why not trust in the resiliency of the American system, in its ability to absorb whatever the crisis threw at it, learn from the experience, and be better for it? Doesn't leadership sometimes mean going with what your gut tells you, even if it means waving off the scholarly musings of advisors?"

The Texas answer to hard times, whether it's a feed store or a bank or a national government, is to take the blow, get smarter from it, adjust accordingly, and move forward wiser and tougher.

CHAPTER FIVE

A STORM SHELTER FROM THE RECESSION

The cover of *Time* for October 28, 2013, featured a provocative reshaping of a map of the United States. The fifty states are rearranged like puzzle pieces to form the familiar shape of Texas. Montana, Colorado, and North Dakota form the squared-off panhandle. Illinois and California are the curve that stretches from El Paso down to the Big Bend. The southern tip, where you would find McAllen and Harlingen, is Nevada. Texarkana is in Idaho.

The story, titled "The United States of Texas: Why the Lone Star State Is America's Future," observes that America seems to be heading in Texas's direction, and the author, the libertarian economist Tyler Cowen, thinks that's just fine.

Those with a low opinion of how Texas conducts itself are appalled, of course, by the prospect of the whole country's adopting a similar business climate, social safety net, and method of governance. But there is a reason why 106,000 people came to Texas from other states in 2012, and why, since 2000, 1 million more people have moved to Texas than have left.[1] In spite of all the shortcomings that liberals routinely cite—our stretched social services, underinsured workers, the occasional subpar school—people are still arriving in droves.

Are they crazy?

Some suggest they actually are. My liberal Texas friends—and you can find liberals, even outside of Austin—are baffled that our state is such a magnet after twenty years of Governors George W. Bush and Rick Perry. They never leave, yet they wonder why others are so eager to come. Critics are so focused on how much we spend on welfare and how many Texans don't have health insurance that they miss what attracts people: we have jobs; we provide opportunity; we are a welcoming society; we have better weather than most states, even with our toasty summers; and above all, our cost of living is among the lowest in the nation.

Half a million dollars doesn't get you much house in New York or San Francisco. It can get you five bedrooms on two acres in Texas. Even if you step away from comparisons with America's most expensive cities, it's easy to see why people flock here—it's like getting an instant raise. Tyler Cowen sums up the appeal:

> The lower house prices, along with a generally low cost of living—helped along by cheap labor, cheap produce and cheap gas (currently about $3 a gallon)—really matter when it comes to quality of life.... Texas has a higher per capita income than California, adjusted for

cost of living, and nearly catches up with New York by the same measure. Once you factor in state and local taxes, Texas pulls ahead of New York—by a wide margin. The website MoneyRates ranks states on the basis of average income, adjusting for tax rates and cost of living; once those factors are accounted for, Texas has the third highest average income (after Virginia and Washington State), while New York ranks 36th.

Well, there you are. So if we can get past the head scratching of why so many want to come here, we can explore why the new arrivals are usually pleased with the move and decide to stay.

Those who moved here just before 2008 must be particularly pleased with their timing. As the nation economically convulsed (right in time to tip the election to Barack Obama), Texans, like everyone else, assumed the brace position. Our oil and food prices rose too, and our house values and 401(k)'s took it on the chin along with the rest of America's. But the earlier oil and real estate busts had prodded the Texas economy to diversify, and it faced the shocks that began in 2008 with a protective coating.

One of the more compelling chroniclers of the "Texas Miracle" is Chuck DeVore, a former California state legislator who abandoned the Golden State and joined the wave of migration to Texas. His insider's view of California's economic self-strangulation gives him a unique perspective on Texas's resistance to recession downdrafts. From his perch at the Texas Public Policy Foundation, a free-market think tank in Austin, DeVore observes that in the recession years 2009–2011, while California's gross domestic product dropped 2.6 percent, Texas's GDP actually increased:

What's remarkable about this data showing Texas' prosperity relative to California is how counter it runs to prevailing notions that California, with Silicon Valley and Hollywood, is a land of wealth and opportunity while Texas, part of the South, is mired in low wage poverty. In fact, Silicon Valley, as important as it is to California, only amounts to 10.4 percent of the Golden State's economy while employing 6 percent of Californians. The mining industry in Texas, of which oil and gas extraction are the main part, generated 9.8 percent of Texas' GDP in 2012, significantly less than manufacturing's share of 14.5 percent—the Lone Star State's economy is more diversified than its critics contend.[2]

And more robust. People are streaming into Texas for all kinds of work, from service industries to distribution centers to high tech, at every level of the salary scale. Is a sizeable slice of the Texas workforce in minimum-wage jobs? You bet, and every one of those jobs serves as a launchpad for self-improvement, a project more easily undertaken in Texas than in the frozen economies of some other states so admired by our critics.

The Perry presidential campaign, which relied so heavily on Texas's economic record, provoked leftist derision of the state's economy on every conceivable ground. Faced with the state's astonishing job growth, critics twisted themselves into logical pretzels, suggesting that all those employed Texans were toiling in misery for slave wages. The liberal American Independent News Network, for example, noted derisively, "The median hourly earnings for all Texas workers was $11.20 per hour in 2010, compared to the national median of $12.50 per hour."[3]

I'd love to gather a roomful of Texas workers making exactly $11.20 per hour. I'd offer them a 12 percent raise, which would put them at a little over $12.50. Then I'd tell them that the jobs are *outside* Texas. I guarantee you'd see their faces fall, because chances are they would lose money in the move. In most places, comparable housing would be more than 12 percent higher. So would utilities, food, and most other expenses of life. Not to mention state income tax, which these workers would have to start paying in forty-three of the forty-nine other states.

The "Texas Miracle" that protected the state from the slings and arrows of the Great Recession is really no miracle at all. A miracle is a surprising event beyond natural explanations. There is a sound explanation for Texas's economic strength: business-friendly policies that attract job creators, who in turn attract job seekers, who instantly enjoy their new state's quality of life.

Those of us who have lived here for years enjoyed the Texas Teflon as well. My stocks got clobbered just like anyone else's, but after the dust cleared I still enjoyed twice as much house for the dollar as I did in the Washington, D.C., metro area, my family's living expenses were still smaller, and I'd never had to write a check to the state for income tax.

Texas is a quarter-million-square-mile economic storm shelter—whether the storms are caused by normal business cycles or by mischief in Washington. People here feel safer from economic forces beyond their control and from the effects of ruinous national whims like the election of Barack Obama.

CHAPTER SIX

TEXAS TAXES, PART ONE: INDIVIDUALS

T he folks at the Tax Foundation are list wizards. Marshaling mountains of data, they rank the states by every conceivable criterion related to taxes: whose burdens are highest, whose are lowest, which types of taxes are most pernicious in which states, and so on. Because of the resulting clarity, liberals hate them. Cold, hard numbers are often the best defense against the Left's arguments of feelings, fairness, and "justice." If a state has the highest sales tax, it has the highest sales tax, period. If it has the highest income tax, or no income tax, the numbers do not lie.

Texas fares well under this kind of scrutiny. One of the reasons we have remained on the list of states with no income tax is that an attempt to enact one is generally viewed as political suicide. Plenty of people in other states would like to join Texas in the no-income-tax club, but any step in that direction leads immediately to the unpleasant discussion of how the lost revenue would be replaced. The only honest answers—cut spending by large amounts or raise taxes on other things—usually stick in the throats of elected officials.

But even as Republicans took the water-cannon hit of the 2012 election, leaders were stepping forward with the courage to say that state governments should stay out of pockets already picked by Washington. In May 2013, Oklahoma's governor Mary Fallin signed into law a reduction in her state's top tax rate, with a provision for further cuts if certain growth targets are met. In Maine, home to some of the most liberal Republicans, the GOP-led legislature pared its income tax in 2011.

When John Kasich was running for governor of Ohio in 2010, he shared his dream of joining Texas and the other no-income-tax states: "Phase out the income tax," he urged. "It's punishing on individuals. It's punishing on small business. To phase that out, it cannot be done in a day, but it's absolutely essential that we improve the tax environment in this state so that we no longer are an obstacle for people to locate here and that we can create a reason for people to stay here." The income tax provides about 40 percent of Ohio's revenue, so cutting it has been a hard sell. But successive budgets from Governor Kasich have reduced the tax bite, and each one has brought him a step closer to realizing his goal: "We'll march over time to destroy that income tax that has sucked the vitality out of this state."[1]

A South Carolina state senator, Katrina Shealy, pre-filed a bill heading into the 2014 legislative session to reduce the personal income tax by 1.4 percent each year until it is gone.

So if some states are finally edging toward reducing if not eliminating their state income tax, are states without one ever under pressure to impose one? In Texas, at least, income tax proposals are derailed as they leave the station. In the heat of the 2012 race to succeed the retiring Kay Bailey Hutchison in the U.S. Senate, a dispute arose as to whether Lieutenant Governor David Dewhurst, the frontrunner, had ever mused about the possibility of a "wage tax" or "payroll tax" to replace the business franchise tax. His opponent, the less known and far less funded former state solicitor general Ted Cruz, used the issue to deliver a blow to Dewhurst's conservative credentials. The wage tax would have been paid by the employer out of its payroll, rather than being levied on the income received by the employee. But to Cruz this was a distinction without a difference. In response to an Austin newspaper's "fact check" of his analysis, the future senator said that he and various allies (among them the *Wall Street Journal* and the former House majority leader Dick Armey) viewed this as a "disguised income tax."[2]

Texas Democrats, being Democrats, would love to have a state income tax. But evidence of its political dangers can be found everywhere. In September 2010, amid a budget shortfall, a poll found that a tiny 6 percent of Texans favored an income tax. Eight percent said they'd be willing to stomach a sales tax increase.[3] Numbers like that tend to muzzle tax-hikers in the Texas legislature.

In 2010, one of the legislature's boldest liberals, Fort Worth's Lon Burnam, actually sought to protect his fellow Democrats from guilt by association. When a Republican candidate for the state House of Representatives from another district boasted of "leading the fight" against a Democratic proposal "for a new $18 billion state income tax," Burnam stepped out to ask that his colleagues be spared the stigma of an idea that was solely his. "I'm the only person that's endorsed it," he insisted.[4]

★ ★ ★

Texas's overall tax burden is light, but there are areas where the pendulum swings back.

With 254 counties full of schools to fund and no state income tax, Texas welcomes homeowners to the world of ISDs—independent school districts.

The ISD embodies a cherished Texas principle—the best government is the closest government. Austin is better than Washington, your county seat is better than Austin, and your school board is down the road from your house. More than a thousand ISDs provide a patchwork of curricula, rules, and taxing structures that leave decision making almost completely in the hands of neighbors on the local board rather than bureaucrats in the capital.

Schools are funded through property taxes, which are therefore higher than in some other states where income taxes contribute to school funding. The Tax Foundation reports that annual per capita property taxes in Texas amount to $1,562. The figure for California is $1,450, but citizens there are soaked with sky-high individual and corporate income taxes. New York offers the worst of both worlds: individual and business income taxes along with a whopping per capita property tax of $2,280.[5]

School funding based on the value of nearby property provides the kind of local accountability that is sacred in Texas, but the resulting disparity between rich and poor districts provoked a legal and political struggle that continues to this day. Property-poor districts faced challenges unknown in districts packed with high-dollar homes, and the Texas Supreme Court eventually ruled that such inequity violates the state constitution. The legislature responded in 1993 with a system that funnels money from richer districts to poorer ones. Quickly dubbed "Robin Hood," the scheme has been the source of undying controversy.

The state constitution prohibits not only an income tax but also a state property tax, so *any* solution to the conundrum of equitable school funding may ultimately lie with the sales tax. Texas already has a relatively high sales tax—at 8.14 percent it is 0.01 percent higher than California's and higher than all but ten states'—but the volume of inbound moving vans suggests that individual and business income taxes influence migration more than sales taxes do.

CHAPTER SEVEN

TEXAS TAXES, PART TWO: BUSINESSES

Mark Perry, an economist at the University of Michigan at Flint and a scholar at the American Enterprise Institute, is the father of a new statistic enthusiastically followed by states resisting the Obama tide. He figures the good folks at U-Haul price one-way rentals according to demand. The throngs moving from unattractive states to attractive states pay higher rates than those moving in the opposite direction.[1]

The 2012 version of Professor Perry's "U-Haul Index" featured a price comparison for moves between San Francisco and San Antonio. If you rented a twenty-foot truck to go from California to the Alamo City, you paid $1,693. But you could haul your stuff from San Antonio to the City by the Bay for only $983. Perry's thesis is that strong business climates attract job creators, who in turn attract people looking for the jobs they've created. U-Haul prices reflect U-Haul traffic patterns, which reveal where people want to go.

So what has created the business climate that is drawing companies large and small and nurturing entrepreneurs? Texas would not be growing as it is or outpacing a challenged national economy without policies that are friendly to business, and that means friendly to workers. What are businesses, after all, if not aggregates of people?

I winced along with millions every time Mitt Romney lost his footing in his race against Obama, but I backed him when he said something in August 2012 that was widely misinterpreted as a gaffe. Responding to a heckler in Iowa who wanted to raise corporate taxes to pay for entitlements, Romney said, "Corporations are people, my friend."

"No, they're not!" came the pushback.

"Of course they are," replied the candidate. "Everything corporations earn ultimately goes to people. Where do you think it goes?"[2]

That seems self-evident, but the chairman of the Democratic National Committee, Debbie Wasserman Schultz, found it "a shocking admission." At day's end, candor had not served Romney well. It was one more item for the Democrats' file of evidence that Romney, and Republicans in general, are too cozy with business and don't care about ordinary people.

So here's the crazy Texas idea: admit that they are inseparably related. Corporations are impossible without people, and people do well when corporations hire them and prosperity spreads from the boardroom to the lunchroom.

Every state wrestles with how to raise the money required to run a government of the size its citizens want. In Texas the battles

get tense because the political spectrum is so wide—from Tea
Partiers and libertarians to Democrats as liberal as any New
Yorker or San Franciscan. Conservatives outnumber the liberals,
but there are still plenty of fights. An individual state income tax
might be off the table, but there is always pressure to increase
revenue by raising other taxes, specifically sales, property, and
franchise taxes (the latter being our version of a business tax). A
major overhaul by the legislature in 2006 lowered property taxes
but extended the franchise tax.

Public criticism of the 2006 tax law was muted, but there are
many—inside and outside the state—who say that Texas's image
as a low-tax haven (an image cultivated by Governor Perry in his
presidential campaign) is a mirage that evaporates under scrutiny.
The *Fort Worth Star-Telegram* analyzed Perry's frequent boast
about his state's low taxes:

> At a Republican debate this month in Florida, Perry
> said scores of people are moving to Texas "because they
> know there's still a land of freedom in America, free-
> dom from overtaxation, freedom from overlitigation
> and freedom from overregulation, and it's called Texas.
> We need to do the same thing for America."
>
> When many politicians and pundits proclaim
> Texas a low-tax state, they're referring to the fact that
> there's no personal income tax and that direct taxes on
> businesses are relatively low.
>
> What draws less attention is that sales, property
> and wireless service taxes are higher in Texas than in
> most other states. Which approach best serves the
> state's residents remains a matter of debate.[3]

Inasmuch as virtually anything can be called "a matter of debate," I suppose that's true. But the only people doing the debating are those willing to ignore the waves of businesses moving and starting here. Critics imply that higher property and sales taxes negate the benefits of the taxes that are low. But it's not merely a question of numbers. Texas is obviously a big state with a big budget meeting big needs. But its conservative leaders have found a mix of taxes that is more attractive than those of most other states.

Sure, a business that needs a lot of land and equipment may face a slightly bigger tax bite in Texas than in some other states. But every business that comes here and the employees and executives who come with it can look forward to more-affordable housing, more bang for the bucks they earn here, and paychecks unplundered by a state income tax.

While there is no doubting the continuing appeal of Texas as a destination for businesses, we did drop a notch in the Tax Foundation's 2013 ranking of state business climates, falling out of the top ten. Pesky Indiana punted its inheritance tax and is reducing corporate and individual income tax rates. Good for them. They're following the Texas recipe, and that's good for everyone. The ingredients aren't a secret. In fact, they're posted on a state website proudly titled "Texas: Wide Open for Business."[4] They include:

- The Texas Enterprise Zone Program, offering refunds on sales and use taxes for businesses in economically distressed areas
- Renewable energy incentives, including tax exemptions for solar, wind, ethanol, and biodiesel use

- A set of tax exemptions for opening a qualified data center

Every state has some collection of incentives to attract businesses from the states next door, or even from other time zones. But after the tax shuffle of the last decade, businesses continue to put down Texas roots.

The legendary entrepreneur Sam Wyly shared his enthusiasm for the spirit of his adopted state in *Texas Got It Right!*, which he wrote with his son Andrew. The Louisiana native and self-made billionaire celebrates the business-friendly landscape that has made Texas the home of fifty-two Fortune 500 companies and twelve of *Fortune*'s "Best Companies to Work For," as well as a hotbed for initial public offerings.[5]

Low taxes are a strong attraction for businesses looking to thrive without being robbed by the state government, but they're only part of what it means to be "wide open for business." Once a company gets to Texas, it finds state regulators whose job is the reasonable protection of the people and the environment, not waging war on business.

CHAPTER EIGHT

A PARTNER, NOT A PUNISHER: REGULATION AND COMMON SENSE

L ike so many other functions of government, establishing a regulatory environment is like walking a tightrope. Over-regulation robs people of their liberties and impedes business. Underregulation can endanger the public and encourage corporate misbehavior. Texas has historically tilted toward freedom for individuals and businesses; protecting that freedom permeates the state's modern regulatory environment. It's an attitude rooted in Texas history. Our land and resources were the foundation of our early growth. Now the state's economy depends on more than oil and gas, but we're not going to abandon the principles that got us here, however unfashionable they are in Washington.

It's no secret that Texans have little taste for federal oversight. We usually see it as a threat to our economic liberties and property rights. Any state with conservative leadership is going to find itself at odds with Washington's regulatory whims. Our challenge has always been to protect our environment, workplaces, and consumer goods according to our own standards, resisting federal attempts to usurp our authority.

The Environmental Protection Agency has become a reliable drag on Texas growth. When Richard Nixon breathed life into the EPA with an executive order in December 1970, he could not have realized that he was creating a monster that would threaten commerce and basic freedoms for decades to come. Under Obama the agency has become a playground for environmental extremists, and Texas faces an unrelenting battle to defend the industry of its citizens.

A state with as much energy exploration—and as many cars—as Texas is going to attract attention on issues of air quality. The Clean Air Act and its various extensions and modifications have set up a tug-of-war between states and the federal government over standards for mobile and stationary pollution sources. The position of Texas has been that the Congress intended for states to enforce air quality standards with a modicum of federal oversight. Instead, the EPA has become a rogue police force, harassing local governments with rules that embody the Left's hostility to human productivity. The Texas Public Policy Foundation and the state branch of Americans for Prosperity make the case that even with our busy oil refineries, Texas air is cleaner under the oversight of our own regulators than the air in states where the iron-fisted EPA directly manages permits.[1]

Any state that stands up against federal environmental overreach needs a fighting spirit, because it is challenging some of the Left's most cherished dogmas. It is an article of the environmentalist faith, for example, that carbon dioxide is a pollutant. But wait, you say—human beings exhale carbon dioxide. Plants and trees consume it. We consume it when we take a sip of anything "carbonated." CO_2 is a part of nature. All true, but since it is a product of human existence, it is toxic in the eyes of the environmental radicals nostalgic for a time before human industry and perhaps before human life itself.

★ ★ ★

With fevered ideologues controlling of the levers of federal regulatory power, the State of Texas has its hands full protecting its citizens' productivity and mobility from the depredations of junk science. But the financial crisis of 2008 opened up another front in the war against regulatory overreach. Congress responded ineptly to the crisis with the Wall Street Reform and Consumer Protection Act (also known as Dodd-Frank), a misbegotten regulatory scheme that gives a curious new meaning to "protection." "Reform" is always a tricky concept. These days it usually means nothing more than *change*, and if there's one thing we've learned since Barack Obama moved into the White House, it's that change isn't always for the better.

Dodd-Frank is a nightmare for banks, which are already subject to unpredictable market forces. Their plight is not improved by ham-handed guidance from Washington. One beleaguered Texas bank, joined by eleven liberty-minded state attorneys general (including our own Greg Abbott), is challenging the law as a violation of the separation of powers.[2]

The bank leading the fight is not a massive institution from Houston or Dallas but the scrappy State National Bank of Big Spring, a West Texas town of twenty-eight thousand.

Dodd-Frank empowers regulators to keep a "nurturing" eye on institutions whose collapse could destabilize the financial system—that is, banks that are "too big to fail." This favoritism comes at the expense of smaller banks, which face higher borrowing costs. Unchecked federal regulators, moreover, are practically omnipotent. "Under this law," Attorney General Abbott wrote in joining the suit, "unelected federal bureaucrats can unilaterally liquidate financial institutions in which the state invests taxpayer dollars. The State of Texas could be denied basic due process rights and taxpayers' dollars could recklessly be put at risk."

That's the language of a state fighting back to protect its freedom and its economy. The suit was dismissed at the district court level, and an appeal is pending as I write.

★   ★   ★

When Texas sets about regulating its own affairs, the presumption that the businesses regulated should have as much latitude as possible excites opposition from Washington and from a certain slice of our own citizens. A particularly vivid example is the controversy that followed the explosion in April 2013 at a fertilizer plant in the town of West, twenty miles north of Waco. Fifteen people were killed and more than 160 injured by an ammonium nitrate blast so strong that it registered on a seismograph 140 miles away.

Regulation fetishists took to their soapboxes to proclaim that this tragedy was the price of Texas's more permissive approach to regulation. The *Sacramento Bee* offered a singularly tasteless version of the argument in a cartoon featuring Governor Rick Perry. Flanked by signs reading "Low tax!" and "Low regs!" Perry declares, "Business is booming in Texas!" The following panel depicts the West explosion under the word "Boom!"

Let us stipulate that editorial cartoonists are satirists, entitled to be as edgy as they like in their craft. But the assumption that the explosion was the result of regulatory negligence has simply never been supported by the facts. The facts, however, haven't gotten in the way of those who are eager to see free-market Texas get a black eye.

The facts do matter to the people of West, and they have pushed back. This little town of under three thousand is a familiar stopping point on I-35 between Dallas and Austin. The town was settled by Czechs, and kolaches from the Czech Stop bakery are the stuff of legend.

The West Fertilizer Company was a welcome business in town, and its citizens—who live within the listening range of my Dallas–Fort Worth talk show—started calling immediately after the explosion, resisting what they knew would be a push to saddle the company and others like it with onerous rules that would not necessarily have prevented anything. I spoke to Mayor Tommy Muska, who said he would resist the notion that a tighter regulatory environment could have saved the lives of his neighbors.

Another snapshot of the West tragedy illustrates even more clearly our independent mood. The explosion was a major story, but not the kind of thing that remains a talk show topic for weeks. We prayed for the lost and the suffering and waited for the investigations to unfold. But then in June, the White House gave Texas a gut-check on its attitude toward independence. It came in the form of a letter to Governor Rick Perry from the administrator of the Federal Emergency Management Agency, Craig Fugate. Federal assistance to the town of West would be capped at just under $17 million. Additional rebuilding dollars were refused.

Governor Perry and Attorney General Abbott, the leading two conservatives in the state, were loudly offended. Perry recalled President Obama's visit to West and his pledge to "take care of" residents there. "This doesn't square with that," the governor announced.

These complaints, coming from a state that makes a lot of noise about keeping Washington at arm's length, struck some as hypocritical. In a brilliant *Texas Monthly* article, John Daniel Davidson noted the incongruity of Texas leaders' "going hat in hand" to FEMA when $8 billion is sitting in a state "rainy day fund" in Austin.[3] "This could have been a chance for the governor to take responsibility, show genuine leadership, and reassert the hallowed principle of Constitutional federalism by rejecting federal aid," Davidson wrote. But so powerful is the allure of federal dollars that even rock-ribbed conservatives like Perry and Abbott can buckle when they are dangled in front of them.

As it turned out, FEMA reversed itself two months later, unwrapping an additional grant of $20 million. But the most important contribution to the recovery of West was the untiring work of residents, volunteers, and charities, near and far, who pitched in with material and moral support, providing the best example of what good people do in tough times.

Relying on those instincts, not taxpayer dollars, is the truest Texas value. In fact, it goes hand in hand with the state's regulatory stance. If we are going to tell Washington to butt out of our business and personal lives, we had better be ready to live with far fewer of its dollars.

CHAPTER NINE

TORT REFORM: A MAGNET FOR BUSINESSES

I t's not entirely true that "everything is big in Texas," but as the twentieth century wound down, one thing that lived up to the imagery of Texan immensity was the awards that juries were handing out in questionable lawsuits. As strong as the Texas economy was, the threat of frivolous litigation and massive judgments clouded the otherwise sunny business climate.

Then in 2002, the American Tort Reform Foundation launched a website with the deliciously descriptive name judicialhellholes. org, focusing an unforgiving spotlight on some of the more manipulable outposts of the Texas court system:

- Jefferson County, on the Gulf waters east of Houston, provided such a warm welcome to plundering lawsuits against defendants from pretty much anywhere that it was known as "the Barbary Coast of class action litigation." Only a meager percentage of the defendants were actually based in the county.[1] The courthouse in Beaumont was a flame for litigious moths, including the half-dozen law firms that pocketed nearly $10 million in legal fees in a lawsuit over late fees at Blockbuster, whose principal place of business was three hundred miles away in Dallas.

- Starr County in the Rio Grande Valley, where a Walmart employee arrested for shoplifting saw her charges dropped in return for cooperating with a continuing investigation into what the retail world calls "loss prevention." Perhaps embittered by her month in jail as the details were hashed out, the former employee sued Walmart, securing $13 million courtesy of a jury that detected "malicious prosecution."

- Nueces County, the home of Corpus Christi, was a medical care minefield. The Texas Medical Association noted in 2002 that 63 percent of the county's doctors had been hit with malpractice claims.

Everyone should favor proper judicial remedies for plaintiffs victimized by unscrupulous businesses and bad doctors. But for too long, jury boxes have been spitting out winning lottery tickets to undeserving litigants in frivolous cases. The soaring insurance rates that such mischief yields harm not only good doctors and businesses but all of us who frequent them. Whatever attractions Texas may otherwise have boasted, medical practitioners and other businesses were packing their bags to leave, or thinking twice about coming in.

The problem did not arise overnight. The state's first attempt at medical malpractice reform dates back to 1977. Joseph Nixon, the former state legislator who led the tort-reform effort that eventually succeeded, describes what happened the first time around:

> In 1988, however, the plaintiffs' lawyer–backed Texas Supreme Court held that the cap violated the Texas Constitution's "open courts" provision and ruled the law unconstitutional. The state's constitutional provision provides only that the courts of the state shall be open to the public. The court's interpretation was a stretch, but the trial bar got what it wanted—the opportunity to sue physicians and hospitals for unlimited damages.
>
> As there is no reason to pursue a claim against someone who is incapable of satisfying a judgment, doctors became easy targets because they had assets or insurance with which a judgment could be satisfied. Consequently, the number of lawsuits against medical professionals jumped, malpractice insurance rates climbed, and doctors were forced to purchase more coverage. And with more coverage came even more lawsuits. The spiraling cost of medical malpractice insurance premiums to physicians was having more than an economic effect: Texans were losing access to health care professionals as doctors left the profession or fled the state.[2]

Nixon recalls in chilling detail the sad state of affairs before reformers rode in to the rescue: one-fourth of all doctors saddled with malpractice claims, 85 percent of which failed; $50,000 legal bills to bat away even the failed suits; class-action defendants settling as soon as a trial judge certified the class rather than roll the dice with an out-of-control court system; forum shopping for counties known for soft judges and swayable juries; innocent property owners held responsible for the actions of trespassing criminals.

The failure of the first attempt at tort reform condemned many Texans to several more years of inadequate medical care as the state's legal system continued to scare off the new doctors whom the growing state desperately needed. Then in 2003, Republicans took over the state House of Representatives for the first time since Reconstruction. Governor Perry seized the opportunity and made medical malpractice reform a top priority. After marathon debates in both houses, the state legislature passed House Bill 4, a sweeping set of reforms that restored balance not just to medical lawsuits but to court cases affecting business in general. The voters of Texas followed up promptly by approving an amendment to the constitution that overturned that 1988 state supreme court decision that had killed the earlier reform.

HB 4 restored common sense to a system warped by corruption and greed. Liability was limited to the individuals actually at fault, and their liability was limited to their degree of fault. The reform ended the abusive practice of awarding so-called "phantom damages," by which plaintiffs were reimbursed for hypothetical medical bills rather than the bills they actually incurred.[3]

In an editorial titled "Ten-Gallon Tort Reform," the *Wall Street Journal* singled out Texas's reform effort for praise. HB 4 "stands out for its sheer scope," they said, covering "everything from class-action certification and appeal bonds to product liability and proportionate responsibility.... A modified version of 'loser pays' has even been included, the better to nudge litigants toward making and accepting reasonable settlement offers instead of pursuing costly trials."[4]

The *Journal* properly noted that such reforms do not arise by happy accident: "[L]egal reform didn't happen in Texas because its politically powerful and well-heeled plaintiffs' attorneys developed a conscience. It happened in large part because Texans started putting Republicans in office. The Democratic Party/trial attorney co-dependency is well-known in Washington. But in Texas, their coziness is legendary. For decades the Texas tort bar had its way with the Democrat-controlled legislature and many courts around the state, which elects its judges."

So has a decade of tort reform worked? Ask the doctors and other businesses pouring into Texas since its passage.[5] Areas starved for medical professionals now enjoy better healthcare with the influx of providers. The Heritage Foundation calls tort reform the "foundation of the Texas economic miracle," and it has been credited for almost 10 percent of the state's economic growth.[6]

Joe Nixon offers what may be the most eloquent testimony to the benefits of tort reform. "In 2003," he notes, "Texas physicians were paying about the same malpractice rates as were doctors in New York....A crisis in access to health care was facing both states." By late 2012, malpractice insurance rates had fallen by 60 percent in Texas. In New York, where the law incentivizes frivolous lawsuits, malpractice premiums had increased by 60 percent, and two thousand physicians had moved to Texas.[7]

Low taxes, sensible regulation, and limited government will take any state a long way toward prosperity. But if businesses and

PART III

FUELING
THE FUTURE

CHAPTER TEN

COWBOYS, CATTLE, AND COTTON: TEXAS BEFORE OIL

B efore we had oil, we had lumber, cotton, and cows. And bison. Texas Indian tribes like the Apache, Comanche, Kiowa, and Tonkawa had been hunting buffalo for their entire history. But when settlers discovered there was value in the meat and hide of those creatures, their efficient weapons and enthusiastic harvesting led to the near extinction of Texas bison in the years following the Civil War. In 1874 in Fort Worth, two hundred thousand hides were auctioned every day or two.[1] The following year, the legislature moved to protect the bison, an initiative that spread to other states where they had nearly been eradicated.

Meanwhile, the Texas cattle industry was enjoying its original boom. After the Civil War, there was enormous demand for Texas beef in the north, where local livestock had been depleted to feed Union troops. A longhorn that cost a rancher as little as three to six dollars could fetch thirty to forty at northern slaughterhouses.[2] Industrious Texans jumped into the market, driving twenty million head of cattle in twenty years up the Chisholm Trail and other routes to Kansas for distribution to stockyards in Chicago and the Northeast.

The Texas Historical Commission provides an online Chisholm Trail travel guide for those wishing to visit the realm of the cattle industry pioneers. It begins with an excerpt from Texas poet Berta Hart Nance's 1932 work, "Cattle": "Other states were carved or born / Texas grew from hide and horn."[3]

Anyone with the time and gas money can trace the wagon tracks of Chisholm travelers from the Mexican border to San Antonio to Fort Worth and across the Oklahoma border northward. It is sobering to think of the time and effort necessary to steward herd after herd across those dusty miles. One journey could supply a lifetime of stories, from the hardships and hazards of the trail itself to the respites and celebrations at cow-town stops along the way.

The era of the cattle drive, spanning the decades between the end of the Civil War and the industrial leaps of the turn of the century, produced one of our culture's most powerful and enduring images—the cowboy—and has likely been depicted in American literature, film, and television more than any other epoch. And it was the dawn of Texas's economic prominence in a maturing America.

★ ★ ★

The familiar image of Texas is of vast, sparse plains, and we have plenty. Long stretches of the drive to El Paso call to mind pictures from the surface of Mars. But the dense woods of East Texas from Houston northward along the Louisiana border nurtured a lumber industry that emerged in the years between statehood, in 1845, and the Civil War. By 1880, a growing railroad network was the catalyst for a boom in Texas lumber that lasted until the Great Depression. At the turn of the twentieth century, lumber and forest products were the state's largest industry.[4]

In fact, the state's first multimillion-dollar industry was a lumber company owned by "The Prince of the Pines," John Henry Kirby. He made enough profit in lumber to build the Gulf, Beaumont, and Kansas City Railroad, which he subsequently sold to finance more land purchases.

★ ★ ★

The hardships of the cowboy's life are the stuff of legend, and working in the timber industry was fraught with hazards. But on a scorching summer day in Texas, we should all think of what life was like for cotton pickers, especially in the late nineteenth century.

I approach this with a head full of stories from my father, born into a family of six kids in rural North Carolina during the Depression. He and his two brothers and three sisters worked alongside my grandparents in the cotton and peanut fields as sharecroppers. The grueling work bred a certain family togetherness, he told me, but it also bred a desire to escape that environment as quickly as possible. It was the kind of life that led girls to seek husbands at the first cusp of adulthood, if not before, and led young men, including my dad and his brothers, to sign up for the military on their eighteenth birthdays, if not before.

If your relatives don't have cotton-picking stories of their own, you might revisit one of the best movies of the 1980s, a story of the Texas cotton fields that secured a second Oscar for Sally Field—*Places in the Heart*. She gives an unforgettable performance as Edna Spalding, a Depression-era widow whose family heroically attempts to scrape out a living in the dusty cotton fields near Waxahachie. The film's depiction of their backbreaking work in brutal heat should leave viewers with an appreciation of the countless souls who labored in the fields of Texas before the broad availability of mechanical pickers.

America is the world's chief exporter of cotton, and Texas is the top cotton state. The harvest no longer requires torturous manual labor, but it is useful to recall the working conditions of a century ago as we turn to the industry that made Texas an economic superpower. That industry was born on the tenth day of the twentieth century on Spindletop Hill in Beaumont.

CHAPTER ELEVEN

FROM SPINDLETOP TO THE SPACE AGE

There is a certain poetry to the history of 1901. The Oldsmobile Curved Dash Runabout, the first mass-produced automobile, hit the streets, seven years before Henry Ford's Model T. It ran on the gasoline that would power mankind's travels for the century to follow and beyond. As the launch of the Runabout drew near, an explosion of oil from a Southeast Texas salt dome signaled the beginning of the state's oil boom, established oil as a major factor in the American economy, and nudged the world into the era of petroleum as a vital commodity not just for fuels but for the manufacture of countless other products.

The Spindletop strike was the product of the work of an exploration engineer born in Croatia in what was then the Austro-Hungarian Empire. When Antun Lucic immigrated to the United States, his name met the common fate of Americanization. Now dubbed Anthony Lucas, he followed his curiosity to the Gulf Coast, driven by a belief that the salty, sulfurous sediments of the region were hiding oil far below. Partnering with the geologist-landowner Pattillo Higgins, Lucas oversaw drilling at Spindletop Hill. It was as frustrating as it was expensive. As the nation welcomed the twentieth century on New Year's Day 1901, the entrepreneurs and rig workers at Spindletop wondered if the time and money devoted to the site would amount to nothing.

An oil strike is a thing of violent beauty. On January 10, the ground at Spindletop rumbled as mud and sludge bubbled out, accompanied by the hiss of natural gas, and finally oil—an enormous plume shooting two hundred feet into the sky. Nearly one million barrels roared out of the earth in the nine days needed to cap Lucas's gusher. At forty-two gallons to the barrel, that's a lot of oil spilled before the historic well could be brought under control. Many millions more would follow—over seventeen million in 1902.[1] Wells began to multiply, as did land values. Beaumont's population mushroomed with waves of adventurous drillers and speculators.

Fortunes were made, but some were lost. In a preview of the dynamo Texas would become in a variety of industries, the oil industry was born on the rolled dice of risk takers willing to cast their fate in a state offering not the promise but the possibility of great prosperity. That prosperity extended not just to oil executives at new titans like Gulf Oil and Texaco but to the ancillary businesses that sprang up around the productive wells in nearly every region of the state. "Big Oil," as it is known today, became big with exploration successes in Texas and California, as well as Oklahoma, Louisiana, and Arkansas. Spindletop, which dried up quickly after bursting on the scene, began producing again in 1927.

The "Roaring Twenties" fell silent in October 1929 when the stock market crashed, though Texas's energy economy provided some protection. The oil boom did not prevent the Great Depression from hitting Texas, but it surely delayed it. Oil production, railroad expansion, and cattle and poultry sales hummed along. Houston was particularly resilient thanks to refinery construction and a growing port that would soon become one of the world's busiest.[2]

Oil was, and is, far more than a financial jewel in the Texas crown. At the time of the state's oil ascendancy, it was a slice of the American economy that was uniquely ours. Other states had oil, but as Texas surpassed California as an oil state, there was a commensurate decrease in the share of influence of Eastern powers like John D. Rockefeller's Standard Oil. East Texas oilfield discoveries, coupled with continuing Oklahoma oil strikes, led to the emergence of recession-resistant Dallas as the oil industry's financial center.

As the Depression lifted and World War II ensued, the growing cities of Texas spawned a diversified economy. The rest of the nation, however, began to create and consume a mythology of Texas oil wealth that inspired magazine articles and movies like *Giant* (1956). Long after oil had settled in as just one of the state's lucrative industries, the story of a fictional Texas oil family became one of the most-watched TV shows of all time. *Dallas*, which led America to believe that most Texan backyards feature an oil derrick and at least a few head of cattle, wove its story lines through the decade of the 1980s. Like all stereotypes, these characters born of oil dollars contain some measure of accuracy. Their appeal stems in part from a fascination with anything that can make so many people so rich so fast.

Those riches have flowed down through the generations, funding universities, hospitals, and "America's Team." The Dallas Cowboys' founding owner, Clint Murchison, was able to write a check to join the National Football League because of oil money, which seems only fitting. The Murchison family eventually handed the team over to another energy tycoon, Jerry Jones. Despite the team's mixed record under Jones, there is no denying his business acumen. He got himself one of the world's most eye-popping and lucrative stadiums, and the team has generated massive profits both in seasons of Super Bowls and long patches of mediocrity. Jones started out in Arkansas, but he brought his success to Texas, a state where the future of energy exploration lies in new ways of bringing oil out of the land.

The future also contains a type of energy exploration that will give Texas another chance to provide an example for America as it makes the most of another resource—natural gas.

CHAPTER TWELVE

COOKING WITH GAS

Oil will fuel the modern world until extremists chase it into extinction. While few see that happening soon, forces hostile to fossil fuels are eager to prod us toward solar, wind, and other renewable sources of energy. Some of these may have narrow but useful applications, but there is currently no prospect for renewables to seriously threaten oil's role in powering our lives.

But the cleanest of fossil fuels—natural gas—is claiming a growing share of the energy market, and Texas has it in abundance. The state stands ready to supply a growing American appetite for natural gas as demand for other fuels flattens. The percentage of America's energy supplied by fashionable renewables has just edged past that of nuclear power—9 percent versus 8 percent. Petroleum is still our chief energy source at 35 percent, but natural gas is gaining fast at 25. Coal comes in at 20 percent,[1] with the help of Texas, which ranks fifth among the twenty-six coal-producing states.[2]

Natural gas will be a big part of this century's energy landscape, and Texas will lead in that area as it does in oil.[3] The over seven trillion cubic feet (that's a 7 followed by twelve zeroes) coming out of Texas each year more than doubles the total from second-ranked Louisiana. The other energy-producing states have some important lessons to teach, however. Texas is a vast state with all the people and elbow room necessary to build a colossal energy economy. With less than one-fifth the land and roughly one-sixth the population, Louisiana finds and extracts enough natural gas to place second. Nice job, Cajun cousins. There's a similar story for oil. Texas produces as much crude as the next six states combined. But number two is not oil-rich Alaska or mighty California. It is North Dakota, a state with a no-nonsense energy policy cut from Texas cloth.

Energy production is not driven solely by how much oil, coal, or natural gas a country or a state has in the ground. It's a matter of how serious people are about getting it out. That seriousness is reflected in wise resource management, sensible regulation, and a business-friendly tax structure.

Each state has a different approach to energy harvesting, and the people of each have their own attitudes about how to go about it. The natural gas boom in Texas has touched millions of lives in different ways. In the last couple of years, it has come to my backyard. Literally.

I am a steadfast proponent of "Drill, baby, drill!" America has deposits and reserves of oil and natural gas that can reduce or even eliminate our reliance on foreign energy. I am among those who say we should aggressively explore for more American energy, not only for the sake of the fuel itself but for the jobs and improved national security that will come with it. I favor all uses of modern technology to mitigate disruption of the environment as we extract these resources. But where do we strike the balance between the need for natural gas and the environmental effects of bringing it out of the earth?

This question became more than academic for me recently when gas companies started dropping wells by the dozens within a few miles of my house. I am one of the lucky Texans living atop the Barnett Shale, a massive rock formation a mile below the surface of twenty-four counties. Since its discovery in the 1950s and its active exploitation since the 1980s, it has become one of the richest sources of natural gas in America. I am pre-wired to approve of this development. But when gas companies pepper a town with wells, two reactions are guaranteed from the locals. One is curiosity about their own mineral rights. The other is guarded concern over the environmental effects of the current favored method of extracting that gas: fracking.

The term is shorthand for hydraulic fracturing, a method of extracting natural gas and some types of oil that has opened up previously unrecoverable resources. A liquid mixture of water, sand, and chemicals is blasted into subterranean rock formations, driving out trapped gas or oil. The environmental effects of that mixture—on the water supply and on geological conditions—has attracted a wave of attention.

Gas companies, thrilled to be finding new sources of domestic energy, are enjoying vast new profits. Homeowners near wells are receiving big mineral rights payments from those companies. Smiles abound. But some residents just beyond the buffer zones established by local ordinances aren't so sure. They have read about fracking's alleged hazards, and the sight of a well tower three-tenths of a mile down the road gives them pause.

In the fall of 2011, my wife saw trucks parked on a thirty-acre tract of land next to our house. Our constant hope was for that parcel to remain untouched. We were momentarily comforted to learn that this was not a construction crew marking off future homesites but surveyors engaged in some other undetailed pursuit. I paid no attention.

Until the ground shook.

The next group of trucks carried heavy plates under their bellies that would be lowered to the ground, lifting the truck wheels into the air. Strong vibrations would be sent through each base into the earth, revealing an electronic portrait of whatever formations lay beneath. This was the prep work for gas wells, which might start cropping up a thousand feet from our back door. Welcome to the test of our pro-energy passions.

It's a given that environmental extremists are not going to support fracking. It brings fuel out of the land for use by productive human beings. Give one of these folks a video camera and you get *Gasland*, an Oscar-nominated (of course) documentary from 2010 that portrays fracking as a dangerous scourge. The writer and director, John Fox, must have quivered with glee while filming a man lighting his tap water on fire, a scene intended to suggest that fracking sends methane into nearby homes. The gas industry quickly countered that underground water sources are nowhere near the depth of the rock targeted by fracking. But if even a fraction of the environmental concerns of the opponents had merit, was fracking something I wanted so close to my family?

Our town held hearing after hearing in which concerned citizens probably overstated the dangers while industry officials

probably understated them. Eventually I had to reach a conclusion. The risks of gas exploration, with its chemically laced water
and waste disposal issues, are probably proportionate to its benefits. It struck me as an industrial enterprise worthy of a welcome—but not at people's back doors.

In the thousands of square miles of the Barnett Shale, it seems
there is ample space to drill at a safe distance from homes, schools,
and businesses. What should that distance be? That calls for a
Texas-style solution—letting local ordinances decide. If some
towns want to keep natural gas wells at a hefty distance from
residents, they may do so. If others wish to allow them in their
living rooms, they are welcome to regulate accordingly. That is
what responsive government looks like. It's the way to respect
liberty while protecting the public and maintaining order. Doing
so has won Texas friends and made it enemies. Judging by the
enemies list, we must be doing something right.

CHAPTER THIRTEEN

A LOOSER LASSO: THE PATH TO PRODUCTIVITY

One of the most influential state regulatory agencies in America has a very confusing name. The Railroad Commission of Texas doesn't have much to do with railroads.

It did at its birth, in the last decade of the nineteenth century. Railroad expansion was driving the Texas economy, so the state created an agency to oversee railroads as well as other parts of the intrastate passenger and freight transportation system—terminals, wharves, and express companies.[1] Over the years, however, the commission's authority expanded to cover the exploration, production, and transportation of oil and natural gas. So while the Railroad Commission's name hearkens back to the 1890s, it is now a thoroughly modern and enormously influential regulatory agency. It's a good place to begin an examination of how Texas regulates its resources and industries.

Exercising regulatory authority over oil, gas, pipeline, and alternative-fuels businesses, the three elected commissioners attract plenty of critics who find Texas-style regulation insufficiently invasive. They "often function more as cheerleaders than regulators," sneers the left-leaning *Texas Observer* newsmagazine.[2] Imagine that. A regulatory agency that actually encourages productivity in the field it oversees. Think some California businesses might find that refreshing?

The "cheerleaders" comment appears in the *Observer*'s coverage of a conference hosted by the Texas Public Policy Foundation in January 2013. The article excitedly reveals that some of TPPF's contributors are in the fossil fuels industries: ExxonMobil, Chevron, and Koch Industries, to name a few. Apparently we're meant to be shocked and outraged that energy companies are partnering with a think tank that agrees with them about energy policy. Oh, the humanity.

Anyone at that conference would have noticed a chilly atmosphere on the subject of federal oversight. The *Observer* quotes Railroad Commissioner Christi Craddick's boast that Texas knows how energy regulation is done: "People ought to be modeling themselves after us, instead of Pennsylvania or the EPA." But the reporter professes puzzlement over the suspicious attitude toward Washington's intervention in Texas's energy affairs: "Isn't domestic oil and gas production at an all-time high under Obama?"

The oil and gas businesses are indeed doing well in Texas and in other welcoming states, such as Wyoming and North Dakota. This is *despite* the federal regulatory climate, not *because* of it.

The EPA in particular is throwing obstacles across America's path to energy independence and making life difficult for states that are trying to foster a thriving energy sector. Federal obstructionism is even taking a toll on the nation's security. David Blackmon, a contributor to *Forbes* on oil and gas issues, writes, "Think of the national security implications of the United States becoming free of the need to import oil from countries like Iraq, Saudi Arabia, Kuwait and Venezuela. Think of what it will mean to this country the day that we no longer have to worry about Iran's constant threats to close the Straits of Hormuz. This is where shale oil and gas is leading us."[3] No one understands that better than the people of Texas, the source of roughly one-third of America's oil and natural gas.

The oil and gas industry is good for the nation and enormously beneficial to Texas, which prides itself on its fiscal discipline. If we are not going to soak citizens with a state income tax, we have to get money from somewhere for the things a growing state needs. Roads and water projects cry out for attention across the state, and oil and gas revenues have supplied the "rainy day fund" that will help address those needs. That money wouldn't be there if Texas strangled energy production as New York and California do.

Loosening the regulatory grip on oil and gas companies has benefited every Texan. Deregulation of the electricity market has brought previously unheard-of consumer choice and lower prices. Texans paid 11 percent less for electricity in 2009, adjusted for inflation, than they did in 2001.[4]

In a state with vast supplies of reliable and familiar fossil fuels, green energy has to earn its way into the marketplace. And it has. The Left may want to jam wind and solar down the throats of uninterested consumers, but a state with as much sun and wind as Texas is going to find a way to make it profitable. Again, sensible regulation serves us well, because prosperous energy companies are able to invest in renewables. Wind farms have spread across the prairies, lifting Texas to the top of the list of wind-generating states. Reuters reported in February 2013 that wind was approaching a 10 percent share of consumed power in Texas.[5]

Consider Green Mountain Energy, whose name conjures up images of clean air and untouched wilderness. It actually refers to the "Green Mountain State" of Vermont, where the company was born. After struggling in the regulatory environments of California, Ohio, and Pennsylvania, the company packed up its offices and relocated to Texas in 2000.[6] Its mission was to provide renewable energy choices in an open marketplace, but finding a state that offered one wasn't easy. Green Mountain vice president Helen Brauner says the move to Texas was spurred by the state's promotion of competition in the power industry, culminating in the deregulation of the industry in 2002. Customers now select from an array of competing companies offering power for homes and businesses. "In Dallas, there may be 30 different rates and all different flavors," Brauner says. "We sell green power."[7]

Indeed they do, and a lot of it, earning high consumer-satisfaction ratings from the likes of J. D. Power & Associates.[8] Texas customers flocking to a power company that decidedly does not favor fossil fuels. It's enough to shatter a stereotype.

In its thriving oil and gas industry and in other areas, Texas is making progress toward cleaner air and water and is doing so without the intervention of the Environmental Protection Agency. Not that the feds aren't trying. Constantly changing the goals, Washington threatens states with the stigma of "non-attainment," the dreaded judgment that befalls a state that hasn't danced to the EPA piper's tune.

The state's foremost clean air challenge is the fifty-mile radius around Houston, the site of numerous refineries and petrochemical plants. The EPA expects a city with a growing population to meet 1997 ozone levels by 2018. Funny thing is, they might just do it.[9] While that goal does not rise to Kyoto Protocol–levels of absurdity, meeting it will be a tall order in one of America's fastest-growing metropolitan areas. If Houston does succeed, it will be because of the same kind of free-market ingenuity that has produced a reduction in ozone in the Dallas–Fort Worth area, where the American Lung Association notices much lower levels than when they began issuing reports on cities in 1999. Being the American Lung Association, they still gave the Metroplex a grade of F, common for many urban areas across the nation.[10] One wonders what would earn a D; an A must be reserved for the interior of Alaska. Nevertheless, these people are sticklers for lung safety, and they do not hold us at regulatory knifepoint, so, no harm, no foul.

In contrast to Houston, the Dallas–Fort Worth area has few industrial smokestacks and no oil refineries. Its pollution is chiefly caused by that scourge of green extremism, people driving personal vehicles to places they wish to go.

This is where I live. My travels take me from Dallas and Fort Worth north to Denton County, west to Parker County, and south to Johnson and Ellis Counties. The towns are not crowded, the skies are not foul. It is ridiculous that these low-density rural and suburban areas bear the stigma of "serious non-attainment." But such is the bat wielded by Washington bureaucrats.

Texas must have been designed to annoy left-wing environmentalists. It's a big, prosperous red state whose economic engine is humming along on fossil fuels. We are a living rebuke to their narrative that renewables are the only way forward and that only stringent oversight from Washington can keep air, water, and land clean for man and wildlife alike.

In Texas, we want clean air in our lungs and clean water in our homes. Our companies want to be good corporate citizens. We love our big, gas-guzzling trucks and will resist anyone who says we cannot have them. But Texas was a hot market for hybrid vehicles when gas prices skyrocketed, and I am starting to see electric-car recharging stations cropping up in numerous parking lots. The Nissan Leafs, Chevy Volts, and Teslas won't be outselling the Ford F-Series pickups any time soon, but we like things that work. From what we drive to how we equip our factories, we share the appetite for cleaner technologies found elsewhere in America. The difference in Texas is that we will never consider such choices a zero-sum game. We are not trying to eliminate the fuels that have served us for over a century. Our energy policy is what the national energy policy should be—friendly to domestic oil and natural gas, yet open to renewables like wind and solar.

Advocates for green technology would make more headway if they didn't start every conversation with a condemnation of the energy sources that propelled America to prominence. President Obama is fond of referring to oil as a harmful addiction we need to kick. In a campaign visit to a Daimler truck plant in North Carolina in March 2012, he framed the choice as "[placing] our bets on the fuel of the past" or on "American know-how and American ingenuity."

What a ridiculously false choice. Texas is proving every day that know-how and ingenuity enable historically useful fuels to be used with greater efficiency and cleanliness, while the search for new technologies is welcomed.

Environmental zealots favor "the planet" over the fruits of human enterprise. In Texas, where we fish, hunt, boat, and hike across some of the nation's most beautiful landscape, we have established an ethic of environmentalism that maintains high regard for our surroundings while also recognizing that man is a part of nature.

The marketplace, naturally, provides useful balance. We want to live, work, and produce more cleanly, but not at the expense of jobs and prosperity. Texas shows the rest of the country what you can do if you're willing to challenge the alarmists.

If government acts like a partner rather than an obstacle, the energy industry will harvest as much power from as many sources as is practicable and profitable. The astonishing productivity of the Texas energy industry provides hope for a nation that should be doing everything it can to end its dependence on oil from a hostile Middle East. Imagine if other states—some of which sit defiantly atop huge untapped energy resources—followed our lead.

PART IV

IMMIGRATION – FOR US IT'S PERSONAL

CHAPTER FOURTEEN

ILLEGAL AND LEGAL, PROTEST AND PROGRESS

Having established that millions of people will be flocking to Texas in the years to come, it is necessary to tackle the issue of those who will be arriving illegally. Just as there is no firm estimate of the illegal immigrant population in America as a whole, no one can say precisely how many of the nearly twenty-seven million people in Texas in 2014 are violating the law with every step they take.

Immigration is a far more complex issue today than in the nineteenth and early twentieth centuries, when new arrivals from Ireland and Italy and elsewhere in Europe poured into America. Immigrants from every corner of the world continue to enrich the American tapestry while sparking controversy at times over economics and culture. We often hear that "these are not our grandparents' immigrants," reflecting a concern that they're not assimilating as eagerly as earlier generations did. One place they have no trouble assimilating, however, is the Democratic party, whose vision of a cradle-to-grave welfare state mirrors what many were used to in their home countries.[1]

While census data reveal a flow of immigration from virtually everywhere, the debates of the twenty-first century are sparked by immigrants who have made their way, legally or illegally, across our border with Mexico. Those immigrants are not just Mexicans, of course. They include migrants from Honduras, Nicaragua, Guatemala, and more distant South American nations. In San Antonio's El Mercado, you can buy a T-shirt proclaiming "MEX-ICAN, Not Latino, Not Hispanic." An explanation is offered in smaller type: "Latino" refers to "Anglo Europeans from Italy" and "Hispanic" refers to "Anglo Europeans from Spain." A demographer might frown at such incoherence, but "Hispanic" can undoubtedly be a politically charged term. Just try to tell a LULAC rally that Ted Cruz, the son of a Cuban immigrant, is "Hispanic." Cuban Americans, whose former home was devastated by Communist thugs, tend to be conservative, a political philosophy that Hispanic activists have declared out of bounds.

There are plenty of border issues in California, Arizona, and New Mexico, but Texas occupies far more than half of the nearly two-thousand-mile U.S.-Mexico frontier. From El Paso and Juarez in the west to the Gulf Coast pairing of Brownsville and Matamoros, with the two Laredos in between, the Texas border is seeing an increasing number of illegal crossings, accounting for an even larger percentage of total border incursions.

In fiscal year 2009 (October 2008 through September 2009), 125,000 people were caught crossing the border into Texas. The figure for fiscal year 2013 topped 225,000.[2] Analysts cited multiple factors. Arizona's famed crackdown may have stemmed the desire to enter that state (a valuable lesson); the booming Texas economy was an increasingly strong lure; and finally, simple geography. For most spots south of the border, and for all of Central America, getting to Texas is closer, cheaper, and safer.

Lucky us.

As the nation sorts out what federal immigration policies should be, the Texas subplot involves many of the same character types—conservatives wishing for a strongly enforced border, liberals wishing to open it up, politicians currying favor with both groups, and a business community driven schizophrenic by the whole situation.

For all the talk of the fiscal conservatism of big business, the badly kept secret is that it absolutely loves the cheap labor pool that unevenly enforced immigration laws provide. Because bottom lines benefit from reduced labor costs, the U.S. Chamber of Commerce supports all kinds of moderate to left-leaning "reforms" that constantly blur the line between legal and illegal immigration. The immigration page of the Chamber's website, headlined "The American Opportunity: Making Immigration Work," is festooned with videos and editorials suggesting we stop regarding immigration as a "problem."[3]

But immigration that violates our laws is most decidedly a problem—unless you're a business that enjoys suppressed labor costs, or the Democratic party, which sees illegal immigration as a conveyor belt for future Democratic voters.

Texans reflect the full range of views about immigration. Our Democrats yearn for porous borders that will make their dream of a blue Texas come true. Our law-and-order Republicans think muscular border patrols and meaningful deportations are in order. The people in between, mostly Republicans, favor strengthening the border but blanch at the prospect of actually returning illegal immigrants to the land of their birth.

Complicating matters further is the baffling tendency of legal Hispanic immigrants not only to look the other way but to actively excuse illegal immigration. I will never forget the April 2006 gathering in Dallas of a half-million protesters demanding amnesty and a path to citizenship for those who entered this country illegally. I walked among them, recording interviews for the following morning's radio show. I was convinced that their demands were utterly unreasonable, but I was not there to argue. I wanted to understand and evaluate a cross-section of people whom we talk about all the time but don't often meet—actual self-professed illegal immigrants coming out of the much-ballyhooed "shadows" to argue for the right to stay in America legally.

I spoke with parents who had brought their kids into Texas for a better life. One father told me, "I would face the consequences tomorrow if I had to, but I want my son to be able to stay here as an American. We love this country. He should not have to pay for what I did." This was one of the great kids you hear about, a boy who has grown up knowing of no other home but America, excelling in school and developing the skills and attitude to be a model American citizen. But his presence here was as illegal as his father's. What are we supposed to do?

The heart says the kid stays because he's blameless, and we shouldn't blame the child for the sins of the parents. But if the brain is allowed to kick in, it reveals the inevitable result of such seeming kindness: every would-be illegal alien would know that a child spirited across the border and nurtured for a sufficient time would render the parents undeportable. Who's going to tell an adolescent that he can stay but Mom and Dad will be on Homeland Security's next Scenicruiser out of town?

I actually had radio callers suggest that ICE (U.S. Immigration and Customs Enforcement) should have rolled up in buses at that rally to sift through the crowd for illegals, an exercise which surely would have netted innumerable candidates for deportation. I can only suggest that would not have gone well. So the alternative is what? Continue to simmer in the toxic stew we have created, where no one has the will to actually enforce the law, so we shrug and legitimize lawbreaking?

There are plenty of Texans who see the issue in those terms. But they are not, by and large, running the state right now. So on to an examination of what Texas policies are, their track record of success, and whether they are importable to other states.

CHAPTER FIFTEEN

BORDER SOLUTIONS: THE TROUBLED PARTNERSHIP

So whose job is it, exactly, to stem the tide of illegal entries into a state? Someone sneaking across the Rio Grande from Mexico is entering both the state of Texas and the United States of America, but if the authorities take notice of his presence here, the federal government will claim jurisdiction, preempting, for the most part, anything Texas might have to say about the nature of the hospitality extended to the unauthorized visitor.

The problem is that the federal government seems insufficiently interested in preventing illegal immigration. This is what finds us in the second decade of the twenty-first century with between seven and twenty million illegals among us. If that seems an absurdly broad range, consider that illegals do not exactly raise their hands for the census. You therefore get those who don't consider illegal immigration a pressing problem citing the lower figure, while more concerned voices cite the higher. If we split the difference at about fourteen million, that's between 4 and 5 percent of all the human beings in the United States.

If Texas harbored only its pro rata share of illegal immigrants, there would be over a million of them. Many come here, stay here, burrow in under the radar, and funnel countless dollars back to their families at home. The dollars that would otherwise turn over multiple times in the local economy, helping businesses grow and hire more workers, are lost. Texas leaders know that illegal immigration is a drag on economic growth before we even get to the burden placed on services, from schools to emergency rooms. So again we face a quandary: Do we deny innocent kids an education? Slam the ER door on the sick and injured? We can't even agree on what to charge the innocent children of illegal immigrants when it comes to college tuition.

One of the first things Rick Perry did as governor in 2001 was to support in-state college tuition for the children of illegal immigrants. The Texas version of the so-called DREAM Act (Development, Relief, and Education for Alien Minors) sailed through the state house and senate, but enthusiasm for the measure has dwindled. Perhaps the lawlessness of the Obama years has focused our attention on the letter of the law. Lieutenant Governor David Dewhurst and all three challengers for his job in the 2014 Republican primary came out against the law, including one candidate who had voted for it in the senate. That unanimity probably reflects a get-tough ardor in the GOP base. But if that's true, how has Governor Perry enjoyed more than ten years of broad approval without putting on the full armor of a border warrior?

His 2006 and 2010 reelection campaigns featured imagery of a watchful governor guarding his state's threshold. But Perry never couched his vigilance in terms of stemming the tide of illegals marching northward to occupy our jobs and drain our social budgets. The language was always about drug cartels and marauding gangs, valid concerns but not at the heart of the border debate in Texas or anywhere else.

Perry and every other state official, of either party, can always shrug their shoulders and remind voters that borders are a federal matter and that the best solution is for Washington to get its act together and start enforcing laws we already have. That approach wasn't good enough for Arizona, however, where the legislature and Governor Jan Brewer crafted a law that removed the blindfold from law enforcement officers. Senate Bill 1070 empowered them to inquire about immigration status during otherwise valid stops, detentions, or arrests.

That was too spicy for Perry, who in April 2010 distanced himself from Arizona's boldness. "I fully recognize and support a state's right and obligation to protect its citizens, but I have concerns with portions of the law passed in Arizona and believe it would not be the right direction for Texas," he said in a written statement. "For example, some aspects of the law turn law enforcement officers into immigration officials by requiring them to determine immigration status during any lawful contact with a suspected alien, taking them away from their existing law enforcement duties, which are critical to keeping citizens fully safe."

Let me restate my overall admiration for and long friendship with the governor, because that statement still drives me insane every time I read it. I cannot understand any suggestion that law enforcement officers, whose job is keeping communities safe, are somehow unduly burdened by the responsibility of determining whether a suspect might need to be handed over to immigration officials. Every cop I have ever asked rejects the notion that this law would somehow impede an officer from completing his other vital duties. Examine Arizona's recent history. There has been no broad outcry from the state's police officers to ease the rigors of SB 1070, and the bottom line is the decreased influx of illegal immigrants to the state. This law has worked.

So will Texas ever adopt Arizona's hands-on approach, which has authorized local law enforcement to complement, not supersede, federal law in the laudable goal of finding those who have entered the nation, and the state, illegally?

Perry will leave the governor's office in January 2015. His likely successor, Attorney General Greg Abbott, joined the court battle to thwart the Obama administration's attack on the Arizona law. But it is one thing to support a state's right to do something; it is quite another to emulate it.

What could spur a future Texas governor to do more than simply scold the feds about lax border enforcement? How about a voter base that demands it? The Arizona immigration initiative was always popular with the state's conservative GOP base, but it gave moderates the willies and positively repelled Hispanics across the political spectrum. In an era when Republicans are threatened with extinction if they do not grow their Latino appeal, we are not likely to see a Texas governor (or a 2016 presidential candidate, for that matter) risk alienating Hispanic voters with intrepid experiments aimed at identifying and dealing with illegal immigrants who are already here.

But are soft status quo immigration policies the only way to attract Hispanic voters, many of whom should be pre-wired to vote Republican because of their social conservatism and entrepreneurial spirit? As Latino voters play an increasing role in each passing election, the Texas experience has lessons for 2014, 2016, and beyond.

CHAPTER SIXTEEN

OUR HISPANIC FUTURE

In March 2012, *Time* magazine ran a cover story, "Yo Decido: Why Latino Voters Will Swing the 2012 Election." I suppose they did. If the Hispanic vote is subtracted, Barack Obama's and Mitt Romney's vote totals are roughly equal. But the Hispanic vote was not close—Obama garnered a little over 70 percent.

If the Hispanic vote had been 50-50, the election would have been a dead heat. This is why Hispanics are so heavily courted. Democrats want to keep them, Republicans long to attract them. And attract them they must, we are told, if the GOP is ever to return to national governance. In Texas we have a state that is inching toward 40 percent Hispanic, and it has been run by Republicans for twenty years. So unless the state is locked inside some odd snow globe where the usual rules don't apply, there may be important lessons here.

One of the first questions is whether winning Hispanic votes requires recruiting Hispanic candidates. It would seem logical, and it is surely a good idea. But the era of Republican dominance in Texas has not been won with an army of Latino candidates.

For a fresh perspective, I talked to a man whom one influential magazine has called "the future of the Texas Republican party."[1] Jason Villalba is the only freshman Hispanic Republican in the Texas House. I asked him what we can learn from Republicans who have done well with Hispanic voters—for example, George W. Bush (40 percent for gubernatorial reelection in 1998, 44 percent for president in 2004) and Chris Christie (51 percent for gubernatorial reelection in 2013).

"In each instance, these candidates understood what many politicians often miss—that Hispanics want to be respected and treated like other voters," he said. "We are not interested in being pandered to. We want to talk about mainstream issues like jobs, the economy, education, and public safety."[2]

Surveys confirm this. The Pew Hispanic Center 2012 National Survey of Latinos ranked immigration fifth on a list of vital issues, behind education, jobs and the economy, healthcare, and the federal budget deficit, and just ahead of taxes. Really? The federal budget deficit? I can see how someone who's worried about education and healthcare might vote Democratic. But jobs? The deficit? Taxes? Could it be that many Hispanics are Republicans and just don't know it?

Villalba has a more constructive way of putting it—Hispanics need to hear a sincere invitation: "We want public officials to engage us at all times and not just at election time. Articulate the message of conservatism in a way that is accessible to the Hispanic community—support for small business, lower taxes, the culture of life, the family."

On hearing this, I re-ran brain snapshots of the last few years. What Republican has *not* put the message in those terms? But there may be more to the message. Villalba suggests that when Republicans talk about immigration, they need to choose their words carefully. "Calling someone's child an 'anchor baby' is not the way to do this." I'm guessing "sanctuary city" doesn't go over big either. So as we look for more palatable terms for children who tie illegal parents to America or municipalities that flout federal immigration laws, I wonder why Hispanics who are U.S. citizens are so nonchalant—to the point of approval—when their ethnic brethren enter America illegally.

Villalba says that's a misperception. "Most Hispanics who are here and who are citizens have their own stories of the trials and tribulations that they or their family members have experienced to become citizens. They do not often look favorably on those whom they perceive have 'cut in line,'" he explains. "But it is critically important for Republicans to understand that the tone of the discussion on these issues can alienate Hispanics if it is perceived that Republicans are anti-Hispanic, rather than merely anti-lawbreaker." So where is the magic translator to enable conservatives to deliver a message of strong immigration laws without provoking false claims of racism? The answer may not be to find new things to say but to make a punch list of things to stop saying.

It's not going to be easy. "Birthright citizenship," for instance, provokes visceral reactions on both sides of the immigration debate. The reality is that if you can find a way into our state, you can have a baby here and create an instant U.S. citizen. Many people think that cannot be what the ratifiers of the Fourteenth

Amendment had in mind when they conferred citizenship on all who are "born or naturalized in the United States, *and subject to the jurisdiction thereof*" (my emphasis). But is it politically productive for Republicans to argue the point if doing so sends Hispanic voters running in the opposite direction? We may think we're making a dispassionate constitutional point, but Latino ears hear "We don't like brown people." Sometimes perception is more important than reality, especially if it keeps millions of Hispanics from giving the GOP a fair hearing.

Villalba says he is conservative because his parents did not look to the government to solve their problems, raising him to believe in the limitless opportunities of America, and Texas in particular. He recalls from his youth the despair of the Carter years and the comparative relief of the Reagan presidency.

But how many young Hispanics today have a similar experience? It may be up to political leaders to communicate the values and aspirations that Villalba's parents instilled in him. Villalba welcomes the challenge: "If I can continue to do my job and to go out there and make a difference in my community and my state, I'll begin to be heard. And if folks listen closely enough, they will hear me talk about a vision for Texas where folks have good jobs and opportunities for advancement, where the streets are safe, and where every neighborhood has a good school system. They'll hear about access to college for their kids. And my Hispanic brothers and sisters will hear that this vision for Texas includes them. If a Republican Hispanic elected official can effectively deliver that message, I promise you, we will win some hearts, minds, and new voters."

Compare this tone with the familiar liberal strains of the Castro brothers of San Antonio. Joaquin is the freshman congressman from the Twentieth District; his identical twin brother,

Julian, is the mayor of San Antonio tapped by President Obama to serve as the secretary of housing and urban development. Those are impressive achievements by a noteworthy pair of gentlemen, but their message is the same kind of grievance-based statism that the Democrats peddle to every other ethnic group.

If leaders like Jason Villalba can show by their example how much more the conservative principles of freedom, family, and opportunity have to offer Hispanics than dependency on big government does, then the Latino vote need not be lost in Texas or anywhere else.

As the 2014 primary season drew near, the early steps of this process could be seen in a Gallup poll comparing Texas Hispanics with those in other states.

Nationally, Latino voters skew Democrat by a 30 percent margin, 51–21. But in Texas, the gap is merely 19 percent.[3]

Even more notably, Hispanics leaning Republican have increased from 23 to 27 percent since the Obama election year of 2008, with Democrat party identification dropping from 53 to 46 in that same span.

Gallup concluded that while Hispanic populations in Texas are rising, their political participation is low. This presents a challenge for both Democrats looking to use Hispanics to turn Texas blue and Republicans looking to expand their Latino base. But it is no small thing that even as Texas begins its third decade of Republican domination, Hispanic populations are leaning gradually toward the GOP, even during the Obama era.

Meanwhile, Texas is attracting new arrivals of all races, as black and Asian Americans learn that Texas offers them brighter opportunities as well. Anyone who doubts the state's diversity needs to hop a plane down here, pick a city, and pay a visit to learn otherwise.

CHAPTER SEVENTEEN

THE TEXAS TAPESTRY

November 2013 was a time-machine journey for all of us who live in or near Dallas. The fiftieth anniversary of the assassination of John F. Kennedy took us back to a day that changed history, but it also took us back to Texas culture, fashion, and society of the early 1960s. As local newspapers and TV stations cranked out images of every aspect of life at the time, I found myself thinking about the Texas in which President Kennedy's plane landed—a place where he had some friends and some enemies, a world of race relations that seems jarringly archaic today.

I was barely six and an ocean away, thanks to my father's Air Force assignment to London. I do not have the memories of people slightly older, who recall school days interrupted by a teacher or public address system announcing that the president had been shot.

Racial justice came painfully slow for those waiting for it, but in the history of human enlightenment, this chapter moves at a brisk pace. Two months before I was born, President Eisenhower had to call in the National Guard so that black students could walk into a high school in Little Rock, Arkansas. By the time I was thirteen, the most popular TV show in America, *All in the Family*, proved that racism had become worthy of lampoon. Against the backdrop of history, that is a hiccup.

Here in Dallas, the fiftieth-anniversary coverage featured hours of old television footage. As I watched JFK's final speech in Fort Worth before he boarded Air Force One for Love Field in Dallas, a particular figure aroused my curiosity. A young black man, he stood behind the president and the other guests at the long head table, taking plates and refilling coffee. I wondered whether he might still be alive. What were his memories? How inspiring was it for him to stand close to the president who was expected to sign the Civil Rights Act the following year? Did the president's visit bring hope to working-class blacks who lived with some profound racism in Dallas at the time?

In the Dallas County Records Building today, just across Dealey Plaza from the old Texas School Book Depository, a water fountain from the period has been preserved as a museum piece of sorts. Faded letters are barely visible on the marble wall behind the fountain: "Whites Only."

Much of the twentieth century featured an African American migration out of the South that had once enslaved them into the supposedly friendlier cities of the North. In this century, the pendulum is swinging back, as black populations in Texas are growing. The inner cities of Detroit, Chicago, and other one-time havens have collapsed into dysfunction. From Atlanta to Charlotte and west to Dallas and Houston, African Americans have found warmer temperatures and a warmer reception, especially if warmth is defined by job opportunities, affordable housing, and plenty of family-friendly neighborhoods. More than half of black America is in Texas and the Southeast.

Asian populations are booming in Texas as well. Forty years ago, Asians in Texas were concentrated in the shrimp-fishing stretches of the Gulf Coast or in academic pursuits at the University of Texas at Austin. Today the City of Austin's demographer, Ryan Robinson, notes that his city's new Asian arrivals are engaged in a wide variety of pursuits. While the general population of Austin doubles every twenty to twenty-five years, the Asian segment is doubling every ten years.[1]

The varied tides of people coming to Texas may choose to live in cities, suburbs, small towns, or the prairie. Blacks are moving in increasing numbers to our suburban areas to enjoy the lower housing costs, pleasantly quieter surroundings, business growth, amenities, and safety. They may not realize it, but they are frustrating the federal government's push to concentrate the population in urban areas.

Washington wants as many of us as possible to live in big cities, abandoning our cars for public transportation, latching onto the latticework of social services that will connect us to the federal trough, enriching current and future bureaucracies. Texans don't march to that tune. We celebrate our cities, but every last one of our major downtowns is ringed by numerous communities attracting people on their own merits.

In Texas, you can live in a thriving downtown, a booming bedroom community, or a smaller, quieter exurb with affordable acreage impossible to find in the Rust Belt or the crowded

Northeast. That choice is yours, and that choice drives statists crazy. All that independence, all that personal freedom, all of those cars taking people where they actually wish to go without a hint of a bus or light rail vehicle—this is inimical to big government.

So it is worth peering into the mix of cities and surrounding towns in Texas, and the choices being made here. Those choices are in the crosshairs of politicians who need a pliant populace living the way bureaucrats wish. The pressure is being applied nationwide; the solution is a Texas attitude that searches for the best place to put down roots irrespective of where the government wants to herd us.

PART V

GOD, GUNS, AND GUTS

CHAPTER EIGHTEEN

LIVING WHERE WE PLEASE

The website looks innocuous enough. The group's name sounds inspiring: "Building One America." Who could oppose such a theme of unity? But as with many noxious ideologies, a peek behind the code language reveals a disquieting agenda—in this case, a plan to coerce Americans away from the popular suburbs and into the cities, where they can be more efficiently prodded toward state-approved behavior.

The large metropolitan areas of Texas boast numerous thriving suburban communities where the growing population can enjoy the benefits of a nearby big city as well as the quality of life more commonly found on the outskirts or beyond. But the Left hates the suburbs—in Texas and everywhere else. Anti-suburban activists are trying to harness the regulatory power of the government to crowd Americans into dense urban centers, frustrating people's natural inclination to spread outward.

Which brings us to the folks at Building One America, an outfit formed in 2012 by President Obama's community-organizing ally Mike Kruglik. Their events and publications drip with clues that they regard suburban living as selfish and probably racist, and certainly an obstacle to the concentration of wealth where they want it to be—teeming urban centers of dependency that vote heavily Democratic.

The urban vote in Texas skews Democratic, but from Houston to Dallas–Fort Worth to San Antonio, thriving suburbs have boosted the state's economy, standard of living, and appeal to new arrivals. These are places that vote more conservatively.

In the Dallas–Fort Worth area, which I have called home for twenty years, people are moving downtown in numbers not seen in decades, revitalizing the inner cities. But around both cities is a growing number of communities that are booming in their own right. Frisco and McKinney, northeast of Dallas, could see 50 percent population spikes between 2010 and 2020 as they mature from cities of just over a hundred thousand to almost two hundred thousand. These prosperous areas have become a hotbed of conservative activism, attracting presidential candidates and other states' GOP governors hoping to tap into the passions and checkbooks of people who are glad to live in the Dallas area but want some elbow room.

Arlington, situated right between Dallas and Fort Worth, grew from roughly 90,000 people in 1960 to 160,000 in 1970. It added another hundred thousand in the next ten years, aided by the arrival of the Texas Rangers baseball team and an entertainment industry anchored by Six Flags over Texas. By 1990, Arlington was one of the state's top ten cities, with over 330,000 residents—bigger than Laredo, Lubbock, Amarillo, and Corpus Christi. Today, home of both the Rangers and Dallas Cowboys, Arlington marches toward four hundred thousand, and none of that growth has come at the expense of the big cities to its east and west.

Suburbs are booming in many states, of course—anywhere there are healthy big cities with room around the edges. But not everyone views this spectacle of expansion with approval. The growing strain of intolerance in modern liberalism is on display in the busy activists and politicians who don't like suburbs (or, one suspects, suburbanites) and are determined to diminish the appeal of living there. They justify their pernicious meddling with a false narrative that suburbs thrive at the expense of cities. All those spacious yards full of kids, all that freedom to come and go as you please, and all the cars that make it possible are a nightmare to the urban puritans. The big-city Democratic machines, meanwhile, are eager to swallow up the suburban school systems and commandeer suburban tax revenues.

Stanley Kurtz of the Ethics and Public Policy Center explored this item of the progressive agenda in his 2012 book, *Spreading the Wealth: How Obama Is Robbing the Suburbs to Pay for the Cities.* He documents the redistributionist compulsion that drives many public policies today, hiding behind concepts like "regional equity" and "smart growth."

"'Regional equity' means that, by their mere existence, suburbs cheat the people who live in cities," he writes.

> It means, "Let's spread the suburbs' wealth around"—
> i.e., take from the suburbanites to give to the urban poor.
> "Smart growth" means, "Quit building sub-divisions

CHAPTER NINETEEN

EDUCATION: HOW TO FUND, WHAT TO TEACH?

I s education the Achilles' heel liberals are always looking for in Texas? They sneer that the effects of those low taxes are evident in underfunded schools hostile to evolution and guilty of other offenses to modern sensibilities. Erica Grieder, in her often sympathetic book about her home state, *Big, Hot, Cheap, and Right*, jokes, "I am a product of Texas public schools, so it's possible that my reading skills are just stunted...."[1] Should Texans be embarrassed about their schools, or is education another area where the rest of country might learn something from us?

The two fundamental concerns in public education are what gets taught and how much it costs.

Texas comes under fire for the way it answers both questions. Calling attention to our low expenditure per student, liberal critics point theatrically to our children's test scores (which we, like most other states, wish were higher), as if they have pinned us to the ropes with the evidence of our neglect. The assumption is that if we yahoos would just spend more, our children wouldn't be so dadgum ignorant. Since 1970, however, public schools across the country have enjoyed tidal waves of increased spending and armies of additional personnel, but with virtually no improvement in test scores.[2]

The folly of equating spending with educational quality is obvious if you compare the annual expenditure per student in Texas public schools—about $8,400 for 2012—with that of the District of Columbia system, a wasteland of dysfunction that spends over $18,000 per student.[3] The state that spends the least per student is Utah, where a generally high-achieving school population happily attends schools that are well maintained and largely free of the pathologies that plague schools in many American cities spending far more.

The differences between public schools in Washington, D.C., Texas, and Utah are sharp, and they highlight what are the toughest challenges in education. The Utah schools don't have to deal with the disasters that occur before kids even show up at school in big-city battlefields like D.C.

Washington's schools, like those of Chicago, Detroit, Philadelphia, Los Angeles, and other massively expensive school districts, have to serve as parent and police. They are often holding cells for kids who are insufficiently cared for at home and triage units treating the behavioral consequences of such neglect.

Texas presents a varied educational landscape. There are successful districts filled with intact homes, and there are the more challenged large urban districts in Houston, Dallas, and San Antonio. The suggestion that a statewide spending spree would somehow lift the quality of Texas schools stumbles at the starting gate.

And once again, the low cost of living puts the Texas numbers in context. Everything costs less here: groceries, houses, and schools. The $8,400 that Texas spends on each student buys as much as the nearly $11,000 per year spent on each student in Michigan.

The most important question is not how much taxpayers are spending per student, but what they are getting for their $8,400. Two useful measuring sticks are graduation rates and college test scores. In August 2013 the state education commissioner, Michael Williams, reported that our graduation rate for 2012 was up nearly 2 percent to 87.7 percent, an all-time high.[4] Compare this with the top-spending state in America, New York, where the rate is steady at 74 percent.[5] In a summer filled with good news, Commissioner Williams returned mere weeks later with an upbeat report on Texas ACT scores. Composite scores were up for white, black, and Hispanic students, matching or exceeding national averages.[6]

This success suggests that the decentralized Texas education system, which puts control in the hands of local communities and individual citizens, is a model not only for other states' education systems but for governance in general.

When I moved back to Texas as an adult and encountered the ubiquitous abbreviation "ISD," for Independent School District, I learned that the emphasis is on "independent." I had lived in states that followed the common practice of directing tax dollars to the state government, which then parceled them out to local schools. Texas wants its schools funded and administered on site.

★ ★ ★

The funding question starts arguments from coast to coast, but they're tame compared with the emotional debates that can arise over curricula—battles that often take place in a fog of misconceptions.

The most notorious skirmishes are over the supposed collision of science and faith in the evolution vs. creationism vs. intelligent design debates. But there are more, mostly involving history, which has become the postmodern playground of the multiculturalists.

The Texas State Board of Education has suggested several changes in tone over the years as books and instructors relate our nation's story.

Take the "separation of church and state." A useful shorthand for the Founders' intention that government and religion stay out of each other's affairs, the concept has been co-opted by secularists to erect a barrier against expressions of faith in any corner of the public square. Should students learn a balanced view that tells of the Founders' devoutness alongside their wish for religious freedom?

Fast-forward to the Civil War, fought over—what? Slavery, of course, but not solely. The South's talk about states' rights arose from its concern that an increasingly powerful central government could become the weapon of a tyrannical majority—a danger that has crystalized in the headlines lately. A well-rounded treatment of the poignant tragedy of Americans at war with Americans takes nothing away from students' appreciation of the appalling evil of slavery.

Proceed to the era of Joe McCarthy, who is universally portrayed as a malignant buffoon on an obsessive witch hunt for Communists. Yet we now know that, at their root, McCarthy's concerns were justified. A substantial number of Communists had indeed infiltrated high levels of the U.S. government in the decade following World War II. So shall we teach that McCarthy was overzealous in his pursuit of these dangerous enemies to the point of sloppiness, or that his concerns were empty and worthy of unfettered scorn?

These three debates have hot buttons on top of hot buttons, and that's before we even get to the granddaddy of all school controversies, the origin of mankind and the universe.

Science and religion follow their respective paths toward answers. They are not necessarily adversarial at every level, but faith is all about God, and science usually avoids the topic.

If scientists were modestly agnostic (quite literally) on the subject of divine creation, these waters would be easier to navigate. If science simply said, "This is what we believe we see, and we have no idea how it all came about," the arguments would be far fewer. But the impression of many believers is that scientists insist on the absence of God. That insistence is itself a violation of the scientific method, which cannot disprove divine creation and thus must have no comment about it.

Young-earth creationists run afoul of this same precept when they assert that all of the signals of an old earth are curveballs from God, painting a picture of an ancient creation that did not occur. This is not an unprincipled belief, but it is not science when scientific evidence is subjugated to untestable larger truths.

Into that squabble comes the concept of intelligent design, which does not require belief in a creation mere thousands of years ago, just that whatever we see around us came from a sentient creator and not by happy accident.

There's something for everybody in that profoundly simplified spectrum, but anyone staking out one position will predictably offend those situated elsewhere.

Consider the story of Chris Comer, who was allowed to resign in 2007 from her post as director of science curriculum for the

Texas Education Agency. She broadly distributed an email promoting a presentation by an author not fond of intelligent design, whose book *Inside Creationism's Trojan Horse* delivers a blistering attack on intelligent design as a trick to shoehorn religion into science classrooms.[7] This is a view one is entitled to hold, but not entitled to promote when one is state science curriculum director. Her endorsement of the speaker implied state approval of the views expressed, violating a TEA policy on neutrality.

But how does an individual, or a state, achieve neutrality on such mutually exclusive options? God either created everything, or he did not. The earth is either billions of years old, or a few thousand. Man either evolved from lesser species, or he did not. The tension surrounding these matters will never subside. Hard scientific answers seem to discredit God. Literal or even partial belief in Scripture involves rejecting some of today's fundamental science.

In Texas we allow these debates to take place. Try walking into a state department of education in the Pacific Northwest with a suggestion to teach intelligent design. Try offering nuance on church-state separation, the Civil War, or Joe McCarthy almost anywhere else.

Many people who fancy themselves smarter than average are the most hostile to competing views on various issues that are literally or conceptually sacred. Texas won't settle all of these matters anytime soon. But a diversity of views will be welcomed, allowing more kids more exposure to more views than in states where favored narratives will never be shaken.

CHAPTER TWENTY

UNION-PROOF: THE RIGHTNESS OF RIGHT-TO-WORK

I don't know how much advertising time the International Ladies' Garment Workers Union purchased in its "Look for the Union Label" campaign of the late 1970s, but it got its money's worth. The famous jingle is still in my head:

> Look for the union label
> When you are buying a coat, dress, or blouse.
> Remember somewhere our union's sewing,
> Our wages going
> To feed the kids and run the house....

If you are of a certain age, the melody may be playing in your head. What happened? How did a feel-good era of strong work ethic and unity give way to the sad state of affairs in unionized America today? Why is union membership shrinking every year? Why are unions associated more with radical politics than with coal or cars or ladies' garments?

The short answer is that we're no longer in the coal mines of the 1920s, needing a union to save our very lives. (Texas can thank the legendary United Mine Workers union leader John L. Lewis, by the way, for driving the price of coal so high in the 1940s that Americans switched to oil in droves.) Unions' priorities shifted in recent decades from fighting for better wages and safety to protecting mediocrity, keeping production costs high, and leading the charge for perpetually expanding government. There are still unions that nobly protect and represent their rank and file without waging war on the free market or teaming up with the farthest fringe of the Democratic party, but by and large unionism has become a byword for corruption and economic sclerosis.

In response to this unhappy evolution, roughly half the states have adopted "right-to-work" laws, statutes that ban making union membership a condition of employment. The name suggests that people have a "right to work" without being forced to join a union and pay its not inconsiderable dues.

If I sound keen on right-to-work laws, that's because I was a union member against my will for four years. Excited to get a talk show gig in Washington, D.C., in 1990, I quickly discovered that I had to join the American Federation of Television and Radio Artists in order to report for work. I had suffered no such affront when I worked in West Virginia, Florida, and Tennessee. I suppose I knew it was coming, but when it happened, it was an eye-opener. I shared my dim view of this requirement with colleagues in D.C. and around the country, and many thought I was out of my mind. "What will you do if you're fired?" one asked. My plan involved not doing anything to earn that fate, I replied. But I reminded myself that this was radio, where entire air staffs are often blown away on a corporate whim. I knew that, because that's what had happened to me weeks earlier in Tampa. The company I worked for decided to change the station format to something that did not involve talk show hosts. They had every right to make that decision, and they were good enough to give the ejected employees a severance payment as a bridge to that next gig, even workers who had been in the building as briefly as my twelve weeks.

I needed no union protection then, and I didn't want it thereafter, especially with the obligation of paying heavy dues. But there was no choice in the matter, so I ponied up. That was the last position I held before moving to Texas, where a right-to-work law had been passed the previous year. I do not envision enduring mandatory union membership ever again. No employer in Texas may deny a job to an employee who declines union membership. No union dues may be withheld without the worker's consent. At the same time, the law protects workers who want to organize a union.

My beef with unions is that they take money from their members (involuntarily, if they're not in a right-to-work state) and spend it on causes that the members might not embrace. If the employer needs to downsize, the union tries to stop it irrespective of market conditions. Nothing—not the business climate, not the employer's product or service, not the financial health of the company—matters as much as perpetuating every job at the highest salary possible. This may seem beneficial to workers in the short term, but the employer will hire fewer people in the long run if its budget is busted.

One of the most powerful magnets of the Texas economy is an employer's ability to hire motivated workers whom it can deal with individually, establishing a bond based on trust rather than coercion. But doesn't the employer's freedom suppress wages? Aren't the beleaguered employees getting less than they would with the benefit of union pressure?

Actually, no. Not when you take into account a crucial factor—the state's cost of living. Yes, Texas workers make less per hour than their heavily unionized Northeastern counterparts. But the difference in the cost of living is even greater, leaving the Texan with more after he has paid his bills.

Other states adopting right-to-work policies are noticing benefits right away. In Michigan, the Mackinac Center for Public Policy nearly fills its days chronicling what has happened since December 2012, when the state made the right-to-work switch. The first thing to notice is what *didn't* happen. President Obama had warned of plummeting wages. State Democrats had warned that the economy would be harmed, benefits lowered, and workplace protections compromised. None of that happened.[1]

So, do workers flee right-to-work states for the higher wages of closed-shop states? Not so much, as the Mackinac folks documented in a summer 2013 study. Examining numbers from the Bureau of Economic Analysis, they found a 42.6 percent increase in total employment in right-to-work states from 1990 to 2011, compared with 18.8 percent in non-right-to-work states.

Some things are complicated. This is not. Some workers wish to be in unions, others don't. The best environment is the one in which workers are free to choose. This improves labor relations, improves the business climate, generates jobs, and improves workers' standard of living.

Not every great idea that works in Texas can be exported to states with different politics. But if Michigan, the classic big-labor state, can adopt a right-to-work law, any state can. The individual liberty of the working person appeals to a wide spectrum of voters. There are other, noneconomic issues in which Texas, against all expectations, might also lead the way. On the most contentious social issues, there's more room for progress than you might think.

CHOOSING LIFE IN THE HOME OF *ROE V. WADE*

In Texas and across America, the pro-life community would love to show evidence of the public's growing revulsion at the taking of over a million unborn lives each year. I know, because I'm part of that community. But while we cannot point to a poll showing pro-choicers dropping off the map, the contours of the debate have changed profoundly in recent years—including the meaning of the term "pro-choice"—as people are willing to recognize the unborn child's right to life at earlier and earlier points in the pregnancy.

In the summer of 2013, the Texas legislature debated abortion restrictions—there are seventy thousand abortions in the state each year—including an outright ban on the procedure after twenty weeks. Abortion-rights activists channeled their resistance through the state senator Wendy Davis, whose pink-sneakered filibuster made her the darling of pro-choicers coast to coast. Her theatrics won only a slight delay. The ban on abortion after twenty weeks and other restrictions were passed in a special legislative session called by Governor Rick Perry for that purpose.

This law reflected the will of the people of Texas, but how much of the rest of America is willing accept such modest restrictions on the choice to end an unborn child's life? A poll commissioned by the liberal Huffington Post at the time of the Texas battle found that nearly 60 percent of Americans would favor a ban on abortion after twenty weeks of pregnancy.[1] Other polls reveal a wide and fairly steady spectrum of views on abortion. But if the pro-life ranks are not growing by leaps and bounds, there is growing approval of restrictions on the procedure that was ruled a constitutional right in 1973.

The HuffPost poll asked whether current restrictions are too strict, not strict enough, or about right. "Not strict enough" was the view of 43 percent of the respondents, while only 20 percent found them "too strict." Seventeen percent thought current restrictions are "about right." So proponents of more restrictions on abortion outnumber proponents of fewer restrictions and defenders of the status quo combined. The lines get blurry, especially since many people favoring meaningful restrictions call themselves "pro-choice" because they don't favor a complete ban.

Both sides of the abortion debate are intensely interested in the statistics of the business, and no one keeps closer tabs on the numbers than the Guttmacher Institute, originally founded by Planned Parenthood in 1968 as the Center for Family Planning Program Development. There are rays of hope in their findings. Abortion rates are falling across the country—from twenty-six abortions per year per thousand women aged fifteen to forty-four in 1991 to just under twenty in 2011. The rate in Texas dropped from 23 to 16.5 over the same period. Nevertheless, the numbers are staggering. Let's look at Guttmacher's snapshot of Texas in 2008. There were 5.1 million women of reproductive age, and 580,000 of them became pregnant. Seventy percent of those pregnancies ended in live births, and 15 percent ended in induced abortions.[2]

Those numbers will filter through each individual's moral sensibilities, but my first reaction is sadness and revulsion. More than one abortion for every five live births. For the newly created life, a greater than 20 percent chance of elimination.

Much is made of the availability of abortion services, with opponents lamenting the prevalence of locations where the procedure is performed, while proponents complain that they are too sparse. Only about 20 of Texas's 254 counties have abortion providers, but they are among our most populous, containing more than two-thirds of the state's women.

The record of Texas Republicans on this issue is not uniform. The politician who received the most votes in state history, former U.S. senator Kay Bailey Hutchison, defended the *Roe v. Wade* decision but nonetheless voted consistently for various abortion restrictions. The longest-serving governor in the state's history, Rick Perry, never misses an opportunity to bemoan the Supreme Court's concoction of a right to abortion that nullified the laws of all fifty states. "*Roe v. Wade* paved the way for the loss of more than 54 million innocent lives, with more than a million added to that total with each passing year," Perry observed in a statement marking the ruling's fortieth anniversary. "This catastrophic loss of life is a grim testament to judicial activism, and a tragic stain on our national conscience."

Knowing that legalized abortion will stand until a future Supreme Court undoes *Roe v. Wade*, Perry defines the battle in the meantime: "In Texas, we've worked hard to strengthen our abortion laws to the greatest extent possible under *Roe v. Wade*. We will continue working to empower families and protect our children's future, until the day abortion is nothing more than a tragic footnote in our nation's history." He is not exaggerating. Perry is one of the pro-lifers who feel we will one day regard abortion as we now regard slavery, an unfathomable chapter in our behavioral history, a time when we permitted something unspeakable.

Wendy Davis's histrionics notwithstanding, the legislature and governor of Texas accomplished something remarkable in 2013—they found the middle ground on the most contentious issue in American politics. A sizeable majority of the people of Texas agree with the protections for unborn human life that the state adopted. Pro-lifers hope that the day will come when the state protects the lives of all the unborn, and abortion-rights activists have predictably decried the restrictions as unwarranted infringements on women's liberty. But pending a change in the Supreme Court and public opinion, the democratic process has found consensus, as it's supposed to do.

Other states ought to study the Texas abortion statute and try to emulate the achievement. Despite the baseless depictions in the media of a pro-life jihad against women, the actual provisions of the law are modest and in line with public opinion. Pro-choicers lament the obstacle of the twenty-four-hour waiting period, but that is less than what many on the Left would impose on the far less dubious constitutional right to buy a gun.

The law requires a woman seeking an abortion to receive counseling about the procedure. Anyone who has had minor inpatient surgery has signed a pack of forms acknowledging every conceivable caution, risk, possibility, and ramification. It hardly seems intrusive to inform a woman of what is about to happen when she seeks to abbreviate a distinct life growing within her. The counseling does not phrase it that way; it is a concise and professional process that describes fetal development and the nature and risks of the procedure. But the counseling is not entirely cold and clinical. The law requires the mothers (let's never forget that's what they are) to see an ultrasound image and hear any available heartbeat. When this requirement arose, even I wondered if we were now moving beyond informing and into persuading, especially with the required distribution of information on abortion alternatives.

But many types of medical counseling cover alternatives, what might happen, other courses to follow, and so on. It is the stakes involved that make them so vivid in the case of abortion. Pro-choicers like to talk about it as just another elective surgery, but abortion remains the taking of a human life, inviting a higher bar than other elective procedures. After years of conversations with both factions, my conclusion settles in: any woman able to see a fetus in an ultrasound, hear his or her heartbeat, learn of abortion alternatives, and then sign the consent form anyway— that is a resolved, unwavering client. The only thing worse than widely available abortion is widely performed abortions followed by the regrets of women saying, "If I had only known...."

Moving to the even more difficult cases of pregnant minors, Texas requires not only parental notification but parental consent. I can well understand the emotions and fears of a teenage girl having to share news of a pregnancy with Mom or Dad. The solution to this problem, of course, is not to get pregnant. But the issue is what the law should require when pregnancies do happen, and again, comparisons with other procedures are helpful.

A school nurse can scarcely touch a child without parental consent, and this is proper. No minor can walk into a hospital and secure a surgical procedure without parental approval, and this is proper. So by what logic does anyone suggest that a minor should unilaterally undergo a process with sweeping emotional and moral components along with concerns about physical health? It will be objected that some girls will face dire or even violent consequences if they reveal their pregnancy in an unstable household. A judicial waiver is available in those unfortunate cases.

The question of abortion funding involves much more than mere dollars and cents. Texas taxpayers do not pay for abortions except in cases of rape, incest, or a threat to the mother's life. That's *life*, not *health*. A mother's health is a vital concern, and an understandable motivation if one is inclined to rely on it to seek an abortion. But the exception is so elastic that it becomes meaningless as the definition of "health" is expanded to include mental health. Since the stresses of a crisis pregnancy are surely a mental strain, the pregnancy itself becomes the justification for its own termination.

The other exceptions—rape and incest—play well politically but fall short morally by ducking the responsibility of delivering a challenging but necessary message to victims—that they should not compound the tragedy of the crime by taking the resulting innocent life. Clarity requires looking at both sides of the coin. A state or a nation exempting rape and incest victims does not consider life in the womb to be sacred. If it's not, then you can argue that all manner of other exemptions are valid—for unmarried women, women who don't want that sixth child, women not ready to be mothers for any reason. At the same time, if newly created life is indeed sacred, the circumstances of its creation do not change that status. All of the proper prayer, empathy, and support we would offer to such victims would not justify a deadly consequence to the uninvolved, voiceless party. But few seem willing to embrace the obligation to take sides in these terms, even in Texas. So until *Roe v. Wade* is overturned, we are left with a legal environment that protects abortion, restrained only by the patchwork of state-by-state fine-tuning of that "right."

And what happens in Texas when the federal right to end pregnancies evaporates? If *Roe v. Wade* were to be overturned, the Constitution would be honored, leaving such matters to the states, as the Tenth Amendment requires. Far from the nationwide abortion ban that pro-choicers invoke as a scare tactic, most states would likely opt for something similar to the laws they have now. Perhaps some deep-blue states would loosen restrictions even more. Maybe Utah and Mississippi would enact more limitations. The key is that these states would be able to decide for themselves rather than live by the will of a majority of the Supreme Court justices.

What would Texas do? The newsworthiness of our abortion battles suggests we would be among the states to tighten abortion regulations. But having done that already, chances are we would go with the compromise we crafted in 2013.

Roe v. Wade originated in Texas. "Jane Roe" was Norma McCorvey, the now-converted pro-life activist who sought an abortion in Dallas in 1969 by asserting falsely that she had been raped. When that failed, she fell in with attorneys eager for a case they could ride to the Supreme Court.

"Wade" was Henry Wade, the Dallas district attorney, the symbolic representation of the legal system that would not permit

Miss McCorvey to end her pregnancy. The case went on to succeed, but "Jane Roe" never terminated that pregnancy. The baby was born and later adopted.

Roe v. Wade should be overturned not because of a fresh infusion of pro-life Supreme Court justices but because of a renewed fidelity to the Constitution. The right to abortion is simply not there. The people of Texas and every other state deserve to pass whatever laws on the subject are congruent with the beliefs of their citizens.

But with the Constitution firmly front of mind, let's step to the part of the Bill of Rights that is even more tightly welded to the image of Texas: the Second Amendment.

CHAPTER TWENTY-TWO

STICKING TO
OUR GUNS

Imagine a Texan of the mid-nineteenth century, and he probably has a gun. Imagine a Texan today, and ... he probably has a gun. There is some truth in almost every stereotype. While about one-third of American households have a gun,[1] Texas households with guns are in the majority.[2]

A University of Texas/*Texas Tribune* poll from February 2013 reveals an attitude toward gun ownership in Texas that is not so much a holdover from cowboy days as a reflection of the views of the Founding Fathers. Forty-nine percent of Texans have a favorable view of the National Rifle Association, while 32 percent view the NRA unfavorably. A slight majority favor expanded carrying rights on college campuses, and a larger majority favor arming more teachers in public schools.

I was awash in talk show calls in reaction to the 2012 Newtown, Connecticut, school shooting and the 2007 massacre at Virginia Tech. While most of the media pressed hard to turn these horrifying crimes into arguments for gun control, most Texans saw them for what they were: examples of mentally unstable people's succumbing to an evil urge to abuse their right to bear arms.

In 1977, I was driving around suburban Maryland in a Buick Century listening to an eight-track tape of Ted Nugent's "Cat Scratch Fever." Thirty years later, my phone rang and it was Ted, who had moved to Texas as I had done. He thanked me for my on-air support of the Second Amendment and agreed to appear as a guest on my show any time. It was surreal. Once I got past my curious questions about what it was like to share stadium tours with Aerosmith and Black Sabbath, we settled into a subject we've discussed a hundred times since: the rights of gun owners under brazen attack from those who fear, loathe, and misunderstand the right to bear arms.

In the course of those conversations, Ted made a brutally sensible observation about mass shootings: "Guns don't kill people; gun-free zones kill people."

Nothing emboldens a mass killer more than the near certainty of being the only one in the building with a gun. Post-Newtown, post-Aurora, post–Washington Navy Yard, et cetera, the best response to the gun grabbers is to point out that armed law-abiding citizens could have stopped the slaughter in Connecticut, Colorado, Washington, and Blacksburg, Virginia.

Guaranteed? Never. But guaranteeing that a madman's rampage will be uninterrupted is wholly unacceptable. That's what we do when we banish guns from the places where schoolchildren and other targets for the criminally insane congregate.

★ ★ ★

The passions of Texas gun owners run strong. Most gun-owning households have more than one, according to the UT/ *Texas Tribune* poll. Nineteen percent of those households have one firearm, 44 percent have two to five, and 20 percent have more than five. You may have noticed that these numbers account for only 83 percent of gun-owning households. The remaining 17 percent "prefer not to say." Reticence about such matters is characteristically Texan. It is not fueled by paranoia or undue expectations of an Orwellian future. It's just that there are occasions when the appropriate response to the government, reporters, pollsters, or even a nosy neighbor is simply, "None of your damn business."

It is, however, every Texan's business when anyone attempts to curtail our law-abiding use of arms. Here's a quick rundown of what Texans may do with guns:

- We are a concealed-carry state, meaning we issue permits to carry a hidden handgun except in certain places like federal buildings, bars and nightclubs, public sporting events, and—we're working on this one—schools.
- We need no permit to conceal a weapon in our own vehicle if we are traveling from one place where we may lawfully possess and carry it to another.
- This next one may raise an eyebrow: We do not restrict the open carrying of long guns. You don't find people in the shopping mall with rifles slung over their shoulders, but there is no law expressly forbidding it.

This aspect of the law made for an edgy confrontation of activists in Arlington, halfway between Dallas and Fort Worth, in 2013. The Texas chapter of Moms Demand Action for Gun Sense in America was holding a membership meeting at a restaurant in a shopping center. (Their name is clever: Invoke motherhood and you deflect opposition—who would argue with "Moms," especially when they're demanding "sense"?) As the Moms sat planning how they would demand action, who should show up but some law-abiding citizens. A lot of them. With rifles.

They were members of Open Carry Texas, a group whose agenda is apparent from its name, and they assembled in the parking lot for a group photo. MDA claimed that passersby and customers were "terrified," though not one mortified witness could be found.[3] The only people "terrified" by the sight of law-abiding gun owners are those who have trained themselves to see gun violence as a gun problem and not a people problem. "Moms" or not, gun grabbers are not likely to make strides in Texas, where familiarity with guns makes them harder to demonize.

At a time of heightened focus on "Stand Your Ground" and "Castle Doctrine" laws, Texas offers both. The Castle Doctrine was put on the books in 2007, permitting a resident to use deadly force against anyone who "unlawfully and with force, enters or attempts to enter the dwelling" with the goal of robbery or violence against those inside. For too long, the law required homeowners to wait until violent criminals were inside and acting out their evil intent before doing anything about it. The Castle Doctrine informs every would-be intruder that he might well be greeted by a loaded gun.

The Trayvon Martin shooting of February 2012 focused mostly unfriendly attention on the "Stand Your Ground" defense, although the shooter, George Zimmerman, did not actually invoke it in that case. The law removes the "duty to retreat" for a person who is attacked in his home, vehicle, or place of employment. When Texas adopted the "Stand Your Ground" doctrine in 2007, critics assured us we were returning to the Wild West, with trigger-happy gun owners likely to leave piles of bodies in their wake. We heard the same arguments in 1995, when concealed carry passed. In both cases the fear proved groundless.

Gun-rights advocates everywhere know that the gun grabbers are on the march, especially in Washington, where they have a friend in the White House. Every tragic shooting becomes an opportunity for government to reach into the gun lockers of law-abiding citizens, as if denying them their rights will make one soul safer.

It is not just the White House and congressional Democrats and state legislatures in blue states who make this attempt. Sometimes it is otherwise heroic private citizens. If anything will win my admiration, it's surviving a murder attempt or being an astronaut. So the traveling road show of Gabrielle Giffords and her husband, Mark Kelly, was particularly challenging for me as I did what I had to do—suggest that a wounded former congresswoman and her spacefaring husband are mistaken on gun control.

They are not zealots in the mold of Barbara Boxer, but their wish for tighter background checks comes from the flawed notion that we do not squeeze enough information from people seeking to buy guns. The expanded background checks sought by Kelly and Giffords would not have stopped the man who shot his way into their lives. Jared Loughner fit the familiar profile of mental imbalance common to shooters, but he had never been legally found to suffer from mental illness, nor was he a convicted criminal.

The NRA, other gun-rights groups, and all responsible gun owners gladly back the effort to keep criminals and the mentally unstable from buying guns. The way to do this is to establish a national database featuring the names of everyone unfit to buy a weapon because of a criminal record or mental disorder. If a customer is on the list, there is no sale. If not, the sale is permissible. Compiling such a database may seem daunting, but I notice that my credit worthiness is known within seconds at millions of cash registers all over the world. It is impossible to argue that we cannot create a world where the default setting is to allow a legal purchase, and to interrupt it if the need arises, rather than place the burden on the citizen to prove his worthiness.

The Newtown shootings sent some state legislatures into a dither, losing themselves in the emotions and kneejerk reactions that can accompany tragedies. This did not happen in Texas, which knows that an armed citizenry is our best safeguard against various dangers, from local hooligans to government tyranny. Texas is not seething with paranoid characters looking to take up arms against the coming federal invasion. But honoring and fighting for Second Amendment rights are the best way to make sure no current or future government considers it.

The concept of a strong deterrent is a recurring theme in Texas justice. We lock up a lot of criminals, and we actually impose our death penalty. But from death row to juvenile detention centers, crime and punishment issues are taking on a more nuanced flavor that can be instructive across America.

CRIME AND PUNISHMENT

The old joke about Texas death row is that our system is so efficient, you can see the line move.

In the summer of 2013, Texas carried out its five hundredth execution since capital punishment was resumed in the state in 1982 after a nationwide judicial shutdown of the death penalty. Executions take place in Huntsville, a small town an hour north of Houston, at the rate of about one per month. That is a slowdown by half from the pace we had in the 1990s, when there were 166 executions, and the 2000s, with 248.[1] Second-place Virginia, by comparison, has executed 110 people since 1982.

By any measure, Texas has made the most prolific use of its death chamber. Liberal-leaning states have found it easier simply not to use their execution machinery than to pursue the long legislative process of changing the laws. California has executed thirteen people since the late 1970s revival of capital punishment, and Maryland only five.

Both sides in the death penalty debate can find statistics to bolster their case. In thirty-plus years of hosting talk shows on the subject, I have simplified my life immensely by concluding that neither side will close the case with numbers. There are too many temptations to commit the logical fallacy of *post hoc ergo propter hoc*—the assumption that if B happens after A, then A must have caused B. I could easily point to Texas's falling murder rate (from 7.7 to 4.4 per hundred thousand people since 1998)[2] as evidence that our death row makes people think twice about killing, but there's a problem—I don't know that. I could point to a state with an inert death penalty, like Maryland, whose murder rate in 2012 was more than 40 percent higher than Texas's. But I don't know that the absence of executions unleashes the urge to kill in Maryland.

There are high-murder-rate states with no death penalty (Michigan, Illinois), and there are low-murder-rate states with no death penalty (Iowa, Minnesota, Massachusetts). There are low-murder-rate states with a death penalty (New Hampshire, Utah) and high-murder-rate states with a death penalty—the top three, in fact: Louisiana, Mississippi, and Alabama.

The only way to settle this debate would be to take a time machine back thirty years or so and abolish capital punishment in states that have had it and implement it in states that have not. Then we could make comparisons that would actually tell us something about the deterrent effect of the death penalty.

In any case, I don't support the death penalty because I think it deters crime, though it's nice if it does. I support the death penalty because it is just. Through capital punishment, society declares with utter symmetry, "Because innocent life is sacred, we will take the lives of murderers." It is also scriptural, a bonus for those who weigh such matters. Death penalty opponents are welcome to argue their objections to it—the impossibility of certainty in some cases, the misapplication of justice in some states—but there is no divine decree against capital punishment.

(I would hope we have dispensed with the absurdity of "thou shalt not kill" as an argument against capital punishment. Killing is permissible in law enforcement, just wars, or self-defense. Likewise, Jesus's rebuke in the Gospel of John of those who would have stoned the woman taken in adultery is not a teaching against execution but a lesson to temper individual judgment with awareness of our own sins.)

★　★　★

While murder touches relatively few lives, lesser violent offenses and property crimes, which are far more common, threaten our sense of everyday security. Crime rates are declining in most states, but in Texas the absolute number of crimes is falling despite a booming population. The state has added eight million people since the mid-1990s. But in 2012 there were 30,000 *fewer* violent crimes and almost 150,000 fewer property crimes than in 1993.[3] Again, without declaring a necessary cause and effect, I will proudly note that when we find our people who have done bad things, we lock them up with inspiring efficiency.

Many Texans are amused by the suggestion that our high prison population is a problem. We tend to believe that people in prison have done things that earned the trip there. Nevertheless, in recent years the state has paid greater attention to alternative sentencing and other creative criminal justice strategies.

Funding for local probation departments has been increased to encourage non-prison punishments where appropriate. Budgets for the treatment of drug abuse and mental illness have also been increased. Judges and juries have been delivering reduced sentences. When the funds for alternative sentencing were threatened by a deficit for the 2011–2012 fiscal year, lawmakers closed one adult and three juvenile prisons rather than cut programs that actually seemed to be working.[4]

The search for alternatives to incarcerating teenagers enjoys general support, since juvenile prisons often make young offenders worse than when they went in. But every once in a while a particular defendant will tax the public's indulgence. In 2013, a drunken driving case in North Texas made even some liberals recoil.

Ethan Couch of Keller, north of Fort Worth, was sixteen years old on Father's Day weekend 2013. He collected seven other teens in his dad's Ford F-350 pickup and set out on a high-speed drunken joyride. He rammed into a disabled vehicle, killing its driver and three people who had stopped to help. Two of Ethan's passengers were seriously injured.

This is as open and shut as fatal DWI cases get. An adult would have disappeared for a lengthy jail term. Everyone expected a lighter sentence for a juvenile defendant, but no one expected Ethan Couch to walk away free. He did get ten years of probation, which is no walk in the park. But the absence of any prison time was a shock.

We all know the dangers of locking away an adolescent offender in a prison full of hardened peers. But what to do with a kid of such absent conscience that he can soak his brain in stolen beer and send himself and friends down a road toward unspeakable carnage? The judge, who was conveniently retiring at the end of her term, swallowed whole an astonishing line of pure nonsense from the defense team—that young Mr. Couch suffered from "affluenza," a personality disorder that kicks in when wealth meets inattentive, overindulgent parenting.

You'll get agreement across Texas (and everywhere else) that when parents fail to teach proper lessons, kids can go horribly astray. But does that mean we largely excuse them when they do? Waves of protests said no, many in the form of calls to radio shows like mine. Callers were furious with the parents, furious with the defense team, furious with the judge, and unwilling to spare the young man himself the responsibility of his actions. But after a lifetime of skating under the blind eyes of his parents, Ethan was neglected again, this time by a justice system that would not deliver him to a jail cell. The boy almost certainly would have been paroled after two years, but that would have been at least a fragment of justice. Eric Boyles, who lost his wife and daughter to this teenager's stupor, told CNN, "My healing process is out the window."

There is no state where judges always get it right. Texas, though still a law-and-order state, no longer distributes rough frontier justice. Our still-active death row is not as easy to move into as one might think. The simple taking of a life is not enough. There must be aggravating circumstances—for example, the crime must have been committed in the course of another felony, or the victim must have been a young child or an on-duty law enforcement officer.

Nor is our juvenile justice system the swamp of brutality of popular imagination. Not that we seek the approval of the *New*

York Times, but a July 2011 editorial fairly gushed over Texas's juvenile justice reforms, and the man who provided leadership on the issue—Governor Rick Perry.[5]

The justice that human beings, even the most enlightened, mete out to one another in this vale of tears will always be imperfect. We do the best we can, mindful that perfect justice will come from the hand of Someone Else in the hereafter. Meanwhile, the demands on the human justice system might be a little less severe if more people remembered the account that they must give to that unerring Judge, who is worshipped and invoked in every conceivable way by His friends in Texas.

CHAPTER TWENTY-FOUR

GOD'S COUNTRY

I t's no surprise that Texas ranks first in the United States in number of evangelical Protestants, at nearly 6.5 million.[1] But the news that we also have the highest number of Muslims, ahead of New York or California, might raise an eyebrow or two. Not the highest percentage—that's Illinois and Virginia—but well over four hundred thousand nonetheless.

Our Catholic population is the third-largest nationally, behind New York and California, and our Hindu population comes in second, behind California.

A state that attracts people from every other state is going to get some diversity—ethnically, socioeconomically, and religiously. But our history begins with near-universal Catholicism. Early Anglo settlers in Mexican Texas were required to convert to the official religion of Spain and its colony of Mexico when land was opened for new settlement in 1820. From Sam Houston to Stephen F. Austin, the founding fathers of Texas were baptized by priests.

During our decade as a sovereign nation (1836–1846), Protestants arrived in waves large and small, attracting adherents from within and without. Episcopal services began in Matagorda in 1838; Baptist missionaries arrived in the 1840s. By 1850, we had ten Presbyterian churches.[2] German Lutheran communities began to grow as the Civil War drew near. Many parts of Texas did not see organized religion at all until after the Civil War.

You could say we've more than made up for lost time. The most recent numbers from the Association of Religious Data Archives show evangelical Protestantism as the religious category with the largest number of followers, but Catholicism is the largest single denomination.

Cutting through the statistics, our Baptists tend to get the greatest attention, partly because of sheer numbers and partly because they have a flair for creating headlines, as they showed with the "Merry Christmas" law, passed in the 2013 state legislative session. However seriously one takes the annual "War on Christmas," there are episodes from schools to shopping malls every holiday season reflecting someone's discomfort that someone else might actually be celebrating the birth of Jesus.

Cards on the table: The religious basis of Christmas means everything to me, but I never look to government to promote my faith. That is the job of churches and families.

It is *not* the job of government, however, to muzzle people as they express *their* joy at the birth of Christ. Sensing that schools feared litigation if they dared to call a Christmas tree a Christmas tree, legislators crafted a measure to allow references to Christmas—and to Hanukkah and to "the holidays," by the way—while fending off that pesky theocracy that everyone presumes is about to take over whenever this subject comes up.

The law permits public schools to have "scenes or symbols associated with traditional winter celebrations, including a menorah or a Christmas image such as a nativity scene or Christmas tree…." But there is a diversity clause. Any display must include "a scene or symbol of more than one religion or one religion and at least one secular scene or symbol." So, the checklist:

- Nativity scene with a nearby dreidel? All clear.
- Three wise men visiting baby Jesus as Santa and Frosty the Snowman look on? Check.
- Crèche featuring Jesus, Mary, Joseph, and angels? Nope. Somebody run and get an elf and reindeer pronto.

There is even an admonition that a display "may not include a message that encourages adherence to a particular religious belief." Having to jump through so many hoops just to exercise a little free speech might provoke some justified eye rolling, but there is value in going the extra mile to achieve even-handedness. It manages to restrain both the militant secularists who would drive all references to faith from public life and those who would spread devoutness by the hand of the state.

Another emblem of the faith of the people of Texas—a monument to the Ten Commandments on the grounds of the state capitol in Austin—provoked a legal battle that reached the U.S. Supreme Court in 2005. This case was a talk show gold mine. Affirming my own belief in the authority of the Commandments but seeking to avoid government indoctrination, I split the case into two issues. Are the Ten Commandments wholly religious, or are they worthy of secular notice as well? And does their presence on the capitol grounds amount to an endorsement of a particular faith?

My callers' views mirrored the justices' decision. They found that the Commandments contain clearly religious instruction about respect and unique regard for God and the Sabbath but also directives of secular concern—don't murder, don't commit adultery, don't steal. So with the concurrence of the usually liberal Justice Stephen Breyer, the Court issued a plurality opinion upholding the monument's constitutionality.

Even under that analysis, I suggested that displaying the Ten Commandments in a classroom or a courthouse goes beyond the mere acknowledgment of our civilization's historical faith into the tricky world of advocacy. I asked, doesn't religious instruction hanging on those walls shout out, "You should believe this"? The answer I often received was, "Yes, and what's the problem?" If there's one point that callers have made more than any other in my thirty-plus years of talk radio, it's that everything went downhill when we kicked prayer out of school.

Well, we didn't kick prayer out of school. As the saying goes, there will be prayer in school as long as there are math tests. What did change in the early 1960s was the prevalence of teaching from the Bible on the taxpayers' dime. I agreed with this but have spent a lifetime pointing out that I favor keeping government out of religious instruction *because* I cherish my faith. The motivations of the famed atheist Madalyn Murray O'Hair were quite different. Through the megaphone of American Atheists, founded in 1963 in Austin, Texas, she bawled her hatred of the concept of God and of anyone who believed in him. Since then, godless folk weary of the heavy influence of their fellow Texans' faith have endlessly sparred with religious folk impatient with what they see as a cranky minority intent on purging faith from public life. The religious landscape of Texas, however, is defined not by these battles but by millions of Texans worshiping God as they wish in a multifaith symphony whose many movements should inspire us all.

★ ★ ★

In 2003, I made a journey every Christian should make, and I made it in the company of Jewish friends. I hosted a week of shows from Jerusalem courtesy of the Jewish Community Relations Council of Dallas and an organization called America's Voices in Israel. I made clear that while I am a lifetime supporter of Israel, I didn't want to come across as a pitchman in an infomercial. I asked for divergent voices, even Palestinian guests, and was accommodated at every turn. That week remains a highlight of my career.

Even better was traveling throughout Israel with the JCRC's Marlene Gorin and Larry Ginsburg, enjoying history, faith, beauty, and no small amount of laughter. The graciousness, goodwill, and humor of our hosts filled my heart as we walked in the footsteps of Jesus, visited hospitals near the Lebanese border, and peered into Syrian Hezbollah camps from a mountain kibbutz.

I found parallels between Israel and Texas, which I consider holy lands of different types. Lots of hardscrabble territory settled by resilient people who just want to be left alone. Not long after our return, my producer Jeff Williams and I shared an account of our journey with a Dallas synagogue audience, who appreciated the observations of two Christians who had enriched their faith by exploring its Judaic roots.

One of my favorite pictures from the trip is of a Palestinian shopkeeper who lamented the constant state of war. "All I want is to be able to coexist in peace and make a living here." Unfortunately, "here" was a stretch of the Jericho Road rendered impassable by the West Bank wall. I understand and support the wall as a defense against terrorist incursions, but it was sad to see the resulting obstacle to his livelihood. We shook his hand, gave him a Texas flag, and bought a bunch of Hebrew-lettered Cokes and snacks we really didn't need.

I can't wave a magic wand and solve the problems of the Middle East, but I returned to Texas with renewed interest in the views of my listeners on all sides of the conflict. It's intriguing, for instance, that my evangelical Christian listeners might be more reliable supporters of Israel than some of my Jewish listeners. In 2012, nearly 70 percent of the Jewish vote went to Obama, who will never be mistaken for a firm friend of Israel. There is no great mystery here. Those Jewish voters liked Obamacare, stimulus spending, and the broad reach of government, sharing those tastes with his voters of other faiths. I do not expect every Jewish voter to place Israel's security atop every domestic concern, but it is a curious thing nevertheless that so many Americans with a connection to the Jewish state would support an administration with so little interest in its fate.

★　★　★

My dialogues with Texas Muslims usually involve what I have identified as a civil war for the heart of Islam in America. As in other corners of America, plenty of voices in Texas seek to under-play or overplay the threat of radical Islam. I have differed from those who say the violent Islamofascists are but a tiny sliver of the Muslim faith; I have also reined in those who have believed since 9/11 (if not before) that Muslims must all be part of a giant terror cell just lying in wait.

Objectivity is apparently hard. We would probably be shocked to learn of the percentage of Muslims in America who danced as the towers fell, but that doesn't mean we should look askance at the Pakistani clerk at the convenience store or the new IT guy from Kuwait. My wish for Muslims in my state is that they help wrest their faith from the clutches of those who would kill us where we stand. I encourage prayer for that goal, a sentiment that usually gets nods of approval. Like many, I have asked why we haven't seen a Million Muslim March featuring all the Islamic folk who talk such a good game about terrorism. The answer has been pretty compelling—aligning against al Qaeda in public could prove hazardous to their health.

★   ★   ★

The harmony in which so many faiths coexist in Texas would be impossible without a healthy appreciation of religious freedom. But a Cistercian monastery in Dallas County houses some very special men who appreciate that freedom as few of us can. In the brutal Communist repression of Christianity in Eastern Europe, the ancient abbey of Zirc in Hungary was shut down, its abbot and many of its monks imprisoned and tortured. When their countrymen heroically rose in rebellion against their Soviet over-lords in 1956, a handful of Cistercians escaped to the West and made their way, one by one, to the United States. Within a few years, they were reunited, improbably enough, in Irving, Texas, where they built a new monastery and assisted the local bishop in the founding of the University of Dallas. With these Hungarians, the faculty of the fledgling university could boast some of the most learned men on the continent. When the monks established a preparatory school for boys a few years later, the thousand-year-old Cistercian tradition of prayer and teaching, transplanted from the ruins of Eastern Europe, flowered anew on the North Texas prairie.

Sixty years after their arrival in Irving, the old Hungarians' numbers are dwindling. But in an era of calamitous decline for many religious orders, the Cistercians of Texas have enjoyed a steady stream of young men—many of them graduates of the prep school or the University of Dallas—answering the call to poverty, chastity, and obedience. One does not think very often of American monks, but these men are quietly writing a new and extraordinary chapter in the history of the faith in Texas.

Some people live courage, heroism, and devotion to duty in the obscurity of the cloister, and others live those virtues on the battlefield and the military base. Every state has a military population, but ours is among the largest. Texas has become an oasis of support for them in a nation that has grown war weary.

CHAPTER TWENTY-FIVE

SUPPORTING OUR TROOPS *AND* WHAT THEY DO

I could give you all kinds of statistics about the military in Texas—our active-duty population of 130,000 is second only to California's,[1] and Fort Hood, occupying 214,968 acres of central Texas, is the largest military installation in the United States.

But to appreciate the military's real significance in Texas culture, you have to start with our civilian population. California may have more military personnel—active, reserve, and retired—but of a hundred randomly selected Californians, how many would appreciate the war the troops have fought for a dozen years? California's military communities are enclaves of support and affection for those who serve, but they are oases in a larger landscape that is much less hospitable. Support for our troops does not require approval of every war they fight, but your support seems pretty hollow if you reflexively oppose their every mission.

Not every Texan is a gung-ho War on Terror hawk, but our electoral votes go to candidates who see America's military as a force for good around the world. Not so in California. And in 2012 it wasn't so in Virginia, either, another state with a large military population. North Carolina, home to the massive Fort Bragg and Camp Lejeune, is a swing state. Texas is the most populous state by far in which a man or woman in uniform is likely to get a thank-you for service from someone who actually appreciates the mission.

My appreciation for the mission and those who undertake it became deeply personal in 2008, when Randy Stillinger, then a captain in the Texas Army National Guard, called to ask if I would emcee his battalion's deployment ceremony as it shipped out to Iraq. The nation had grown weary of Iraq, Afghanistan, and any other theater of a war that after six years had not ended tidily. On a conservative talk show in Texas, I could still find support for the effort—and among my listeners were members of the 2-149 General Support Aviation Battalion, based in Grand Prairie, just west of Dallas.

As the battalion trained for deployment, I visited headquarters to meet the troops, go over the ceremony agenda—and fly in a Blackhawk helicopter over Dallas–Fort Worth. Strapped in on the open side of the helicopter, I watched the Grand Prairie airstrip shrink as we gained altitude. We buzzed some Arlington landmarks, including the construction site of the half-finished Cowboys stadium. Then it was fifteen minutes north to another location I knew well—my house. The pictures I took of my property, with the little specks that are my family in the yard, are in a folder alongside the pictures my wife took of us flying over at five hundred feet. But we were not just burning the taxpayers' fuel dollars on a joyride. We peeled off to a stretch of grassland near Eagle Mountain Lake, northwest of Fort Worth, to practice some maneuvers needed in case of a rapid troop drop or a medical evacuation—dropping from altitude, hovering for a few seconds, and then gunning it to get back up.

Quite the ride. What a thrill it was to see the proficiency of the men flying these machines, Texans who sacrificed big parts of their lives as professionals, fathers, and husbands to fly helicopters in a war zone.

And they were not all men. Captain Carisa Kimbro grew up riding horses in Katy, west of Houston. When I met her, she was in the belly of the twenty-five-thousand-pound CH-47 Chinook she would be jockeying in Iraq for the next year. Kimbro was not the only impressive woman in the battalion. Back at headquarters, I met the commander. Lieutenant Colonel Joanne MacGregor shared her gratitude that I would give my time to their deployment ceremony. I replied that this was surely the least I could do, in view of the journey she and hundreds of her fellow troops were about to make for me.

The ceremony was in the gym of South Grand Prairie High School on a Saturday morning, the last day many of these families would spend together for a long time. Kids climbed through the static display helicopters in the parking lot while soldiers in tan fatigues munched barbecue sandwiches in the cafeteria. After lunch, I gathered with Congressman Michael Burgess and the other dignitaries on the program as the troops gathered outside the gym to be brought in, company by company, to the cheering of wives (and husbands), parents, and kids. The walls of the gym were covered in wholly appropriate school mascot imagery: "Home of the Warriors."

No words I spoke that day could properly convey the gratitude of a fortunate citizen in the company of those who would lay down their lives for our country. There was a brief pause midway in the program, and the battalion was given an at-ease before the next speaker. The decorum momentarily suspended, friends and loved ones called out from the bleachers: "Steeeeve!" "Hi, honey!" "Daddy!"

As we wrapped up the proceedings, the crowd dispersed—the troops to buses bound for Fort Sill, Oklahoma, for final training before Balad, Iraq, and the families to homes that would be missing a loved one for a little over a year.

Or for the rest of their lives.

The battalion traveled to Kuwait for regrouping and transfer to Iraq. Around midnight on September 17, 2008, four choppers were churning over the desert in close formation when one, dubbed Red River 44, went nose down.

A year later, I was granted the privilege of emceeing the return ceremony of the 2-149. Families came together with smiles and tears of joy and gratitude. But seven families in attendance had lost sons, fathers, brothers. Their names were mentioned often, and I met their wives, parents, and friends afterward. What do you say to a woman, whom you may well have met at the deployment ceremony a year earlier, whose husband didn't come home? What do you say to the parents of that solider? To his kids?

Ultimately, the answer comes: "Thank you."

The year before, I had thanked the soldiers for the sacrifice they were about to make, and the families for theirs. On the gray, rainy afternoon of their return ceremony, I thanked them for their service, and thanked the fallen and their families for the ultimate sacrifice. A full year after the crash, those families showed no bitterness, no anger, no resentment. They were sad and reflective but also grateful to be in the company of other families and the men and women who had deployed alongside their heroes.

Those families are heroes as well. Three of the crew of Red River 44 were from Oklahoma: Sergeant Daniel Eshbaugh of Norman, Captain Michael Thompson of Kingston, and Chief Warrant Officer Brady Rudolf of Oklahoma City. Four were from Texas: CWO Corry Edwards of Kennedale, Sergeant Anthony Luke Mason of Springtown, First Sergeant Julio Ordonez of San Antonio, and First Lieutenant Robert Vallejo II of North Richland Hills. His wife, Hillary, had given birth to Robert Vallejo III the previous January.

To meet these citizen-soldiers, to meet their families—to be with them in moments of pride and moments of sorrow and healing—is a tonic for the spirit. I heard not one voice of fatigue with the mission, not one voice of discord or impatience with a war from which there is no easy exit. These men and women were glad to serve and glad to go wherever necessary to protect our nation from attack. I have asked antiwar people ever since to tell me what makes them smarter than the soldiers of the 2-149.

As this small story shows, there is a harmony between Texans and soldiers—no surprise, since an awful lot of soldiers come from Texas. There's still a belief here that sometimes you have to fight for what's important, that our country and our freedom are worth fighting for, and that the soldiers who are ready to do that fighting deserve all the honor we can give them. Texans are not the only Americans who think that way, but we don't have to spend a lot of time apologizing for it. That's one of the many differences between Texas and the state against which it is often measured—the Golden State of California.

PART VI

RED, BLUE, AND PURPLE: DIFFERENT STATES, DIFFERENT FATES

CHAPTER TWENTY-SIX

CALIFORNIA: THE ANTI-TEXAS

Imagine you are a Silicon Valley software designer or an LA hipster or a Sausalito sculptor. You are driving along a sun-drenched California highway, and you feel lucky that the traffic is not too brutal. Maybe you are politically active, maybe not, but when the talk turns to politics, you lean left. After all, look what you do. Look where you are.

Your favorite radio station is the soundtrack to a pleasant drive—when suddenly, during a commercial break, a voice with a distinct Texas twang comes over the air. "Building a business is tough," it begins. "But I hear building a business in California is next to impossible...." What is this? You consider firing up a playlist, maybe some Nirvana or Jackson Browne. But you can't turn away. Not yet.

"This is Texas governor Rick Perry, and I have a message for California businesses: Come check out Texas." At this point, the car could catch on fire and you're not getting out. What is happening here? Is a governor from another state actually buying time on California stations to lure businesses away from the Golden State?

Yup.

"There are plenty of reasons Texas has been named the best state for doing business for eight years running," Perry continues. "Visit 'Texas wide open for business dot com,' and see why our low taxes, sensible regulations, and fair legal system are just the thing to get your business moving—to Texas."

You steer the car back onto the road and speed-dial friends, colleagues, and business partners to ask if they have caught wind of this insolence. Finding some who have, you marvel at the sheer nerve of this Texas rube elbowing his way onto your car radio to put down your state. You have a few chuckles. Then, after everyone hangs up, the realization starts to settle in: this man who disagrees with you on nearly every issue has compelling evidence on his side.

Since Ronald Reagan left Sacramento in 1975, California has had three Democratic governors, and two of them have been Jerry Brown. "Governor Moonbeam," as he was known in younger days, was Reagan's two-term successor, and he is the incumbent today. Gray Davis, elected in 1998 and 2002 and recalled in 2003, is the other.

After Brown left office in 1983, Californians spent sixteen years under Republican governors: two terms of George Deukmejian and two terms of Pete Wilson. Neither could be confused with Rick Perry. Post-Reagan California Republicans have deviated from their party's national norm, just as many Texas Democrats have done.

Under governors of both parties, California has been a willing partner with Washington in tightening government control of the state's citizens and businesses. Californians from Crescent City to San Ysidro have elected state and local officials who have pulled the state profoundly leftward. For more than twenty years, their U.S. senators have been those paragons of unreflective leftism, Barbara Boxer and Dianne Feinstein.

It's hard to imagine a starker contrast during those same twenty years than ruby-red Texas, which has enjoyed a historic boom in new businesses and new arrivals. Taxes have been restrained, spending controlled, and regulation reasonable; in California, taxes, spending, and regulations have all swelled—devouring household incomes and business profits.

Chuck DeVore, the Texas Public Policy Foundation's transplanted Californian, knows a few things about the differences between the two states. He responds to those who deny that government policies are responsible for the disparity between the two states' economic fortunes with something they might never have encountered before—the facts:

> If, as the critics opine, Texas is adding jobs simply because it is adding people, then the ratio of jobs added to population increased ought to be roughly the same there as in the U.S. as a whole. The data shows the opposite. Texas added one new job for every three people from 2000 to 2013, while the nation added one job for every seven people—meaning that Texas outperformed the U.S. job creation rate by more than two-to-one. In the same period, California added one job for every 11 new residents. No amount of taxes will

allow one worker to support 11 people indefinitely, no matter how robust the welfare state.[1]

In a study for the Manhattan Institute in 2012, Tom Gray and Robert Scardamalia examined what they call "The Great California Exodus."[2] The study paints a picture of a state conducting a master class in how to implode. The astronomical price of what California has done is best measured by what it now cannot do. Years of living vastly beyond its means will damage any state's health, and now California simply cannot afford to offer the kind of tax credits Texas uses to attract new businesses every year.

Invoking the $36 million in incentives Texas offered Apple to bring 3,600 additional jobs to Austin, the authors ask if California's inability to float such offers is part of a "cycle of decline, in which a loss of jobs to other states leads to a loss of tax-paying residents, and in turn to a deterioration of the public services that make the state even less desirable for businesses."

Ouch.

It seems only yesterday that you could call California the "Golden State" without irony. After World War II, it was the land of opportunity; people flocked to it as they flock to Texas today. Texans take no pleasure in California's decline, because we know that prosperity is not a zero-sum game. In a free-market economy, Texas and California could both be boom states—along with the other forty-eight. Texas doesn't have to be the only state with a "miracle," because there is nothing miraculous about the simple steps necessary to prosper. Political self-discipline can be difficult, of course, but without the will to control spending, taxing, and regulating, a state (or a city or a country) will drift into ruin. The lessons are everywhere—Greece, Detroit, and, I'm sorry to say, California.

Maybe the first thing people in other states need to do is realize the wide latitude they have under the Constitution. With the Tenth Amendment, the Founders left most issues to the states and the people to deal with as they think best. Other states don't have to copy Texas—let a thousand flowers bloom! But each state asserting its own will, rather than succumbing to federal whims, is what the American experiment is about.

CHAPTER TWENTY-SEVEN

TARGETING TEXAS

I f I had compiled an over-the-top wish list of events to coincide with this book's final deadline, it might have contained some wheels-off reaches like

- The governor of a big liberal state says something incredibly dumb, alienating a huge chunk of his struggling constituents
- A major media figure responds by expressing a wish to leave that state and move his family, perhaps to Texas
- A high-ranking Texas official issues an invitation for him to leave hostile territory behind and join the waves of Americans moving to Texas and a better life

- And then, to tie it all up with a bow, a major magazine—*Forbes*, let's say—runs a piece referring to
  Texas as "the most important place in the world"

It's not as though my thesis needs these things to support it. All manner of events were already aligning to show how Texas can show the way to other states and the nation as a whole. A pie-in-the-sky series of events like the one described above seems like the stuff of fantasy.

Or it did, until all of those things happened.

In mid-January 2014, the governor of New York, Andrew Cuomo, began talking about the Republicans in his state in a radio interview. "They're searching to define their soul," he said. "It's a mirror of what's going on in Washington. The gridlock in Washington is less about Democrats and Republicans. It's more about extreme Republicans versus more moderate Republicans." Replace "extreme" with "true conservative," and that line could have come from a Tea Party meeting. Governor Cuomo is right in suggesting that many Republicans feel the party must figure out what it stands for if it is to pose a coherent challenge to the Democrats.

But then, in speaking of the steadfast, solid, dependable conservatives in his own state, the governor launched into a vitriolic rant that might make Chris Matthews blush: "Who are they? Are they these extreme conservatives who are right-to-life, pro-assault-weapon, anti-gay? Is that who they are? Because if that's who they are and they're the extreme conservatives, they have no place in the state of New York, because that's not who New Yorkers are."[1]

The governor's pronouncement came as a surprise to the millions of New Yorkers who actually *are* pro-life, pro–Second Amendment, and pro–traditional marriage. Obviously they are a minority in a deep-blue state, but for the governor to wish them away like a bad rash is a remarkable affront even in these coarse times.

Reactions were swift. "My governor thinks there's no place in NY for people like me," tweeted Dennis Proust, spokesman of the state Catholic Conference. "Can I get a state grant to relocate?"[2] But the reaction that garnered the most attention was from conservative media's most prominent New Yorker, Sean Hannity, who expressed a desire to pack up his family and his broadcast operation and bail from his native state for friendlier shores. "I can't wait to pay no state income tax down in Florida or Texas," he announced, invoking two states that have lured the talk radio titans Rush Limbaugh (now of Palm Beach, Florida) and Glenn Beck (now operating from Irving, Texas) from New York in recent years. As Sean pondered joining that exodus, he addressed New York's new arbiter of acceptable opinion directly: "Governor Cuomo, I'm going to leave and I'm taking all of my money with me—every single, solitary penny. And by the way, Governor, because I work here—there's a whole bunch of people that work for me and benefit because I do two shows. And I guess maybe some of them will be out of work, Governor. I'm sure you'll take care of them."

In case any of Sean's employees (or family members, for that matter) were wondering if their winter was suddenly about to get warmer, he soon made it clear that his timing would depend on the graduation of his teenage son from high school. I could argue that Sean's kids could get a great education at any number of wonderful private or public schools in Texas, but I'll leave that decision up to him. Suffice it to say that a narrative is building, featuring people whose talents have earned them the blessing of wealth growing sick of their bloated state governments' pilfering that wealth.

The Cuomo-Hannity flap rekindles memories of the golfer Phil Mickelson's ruminations in early 2013 about leaving California, which devours an enormous slice of his hard-earned winnings. One could even invoke the French actor Gerard Depardieu, who bolted his native land to seek tax relief in 2012 in a border town in Belgium. Don't high-tax states and nations get it? They may enjoy for a while the proceeds of confiscatory tax rates, but ultimately they kill the goose that lays the golden egg. Their biggest earners decide they have had enough and pack their bags to live under less gluttonous rule elsewhere.

New Yorkers may be noticing the problem. Note the debut of START-UP NY (startup.ny.com), a Cuomo administration program offering "tax-free zones" in which new businesses can enjoy ten years without corporate, state, or local taxes, including sales and property taxes and franchise fees. If this is the first step in a change of course that could revitalize New York, good. But the TV campaign for the website contains an assertion that may be hard to live up to under Cuomo-style leadership. After offering the carrot of a tax-free decade in business, the ad asserts, "If there's something that creates more jobs and grows more businesses, we're open to it."

Pardon my skepticism. The things that truly grow businesses and create jobs are the policies on display in Texas and the other states with low taxes, sensible regulation, and respect for property rights. If New York is going to pursue strategies that would improve its economic outlook, voters will have to start electing different kinds of leaders. That may take a while, but it will be worth it.

At each step along the way, though, statists will fight to protect their dwindling territory. If New Yorkers want to see how that fight plays out, they can watch what happens in Texas in the coming years. Despite the ample evidence of the wisdom of small government and low taxation, Democrats and even our own special strain of big-spending Republicans are circling the wagons to protect the government programs they want to perpetuate.

This activity has drawn the attention of Brian Domitrovic, an economic historian at Sam Houston State University who thinks the stakes are stratospherically high. From his outpost at the state's third-oldest public institution of higher learning, Domitrovic points to the Texas economy as a singular example in a world where big-government instincts threaten futures across the globe. In an article in *Forbes* titled "Big-Government Stirrings in Texas, the Most Important Place in the World," Domitrovic describes the evolving struggle between big spenders and those fighting to stay the course that has made the state "the only notable place on the globe that has pursued relatively small-government policy against the grain of Keynesian resurgence." Texas, says Domitrovic, has "shown the world that the way back to mass prosperity is to let the private economy run."[3]

Such an achievement, however, is never secure. Domitrovic warns that American and international advocates of big government are girding for battle against the state where their collectivist principles have been proved false. They want to end the Texas story before it can inspire the rest of the country. After twenty years of conservative governance in the Lone Star State, the national Democrat party is trying to turn Texas purple, then blue. And within the state itself, Democrats are plotting against all Republicans, while moderate Republicans also feel the heat from steadfast conservatives determined not to let Texas turn away from the policies that have created our precious prosperity.

Sound familiar? It's a microcosm of America as a whole as we head toward a vital off-year election and a 2016 presidential race that will chart our course into the next decade. But while America has veered left with disastrous results, Texans are having to fend off challenges to policies that have been strikingly successful.

Many crucial battles will have been fought both at the national level and in the various states by November 2016. Voters will give different answers on questions over how much to tax, how much to spend, how much to protect liberty, and how to spark growth. Will Americans in other states choose the Texas-style solutions that have been shown to foster a booming economy, or will they continue to roll the dice on experiments in big government? Texas can provide a stellar example to the rest of the nation all day, every day. But if the benefits we enjoy as Texans are to be spread more widely, voters elsewhere will have to notice, learn from our example, and join us on a more prosperous path.

CHAPTER TWENTY-EIGHT

NORTH DAKOTA

There are other states around the country that are singing from the same page as Texas, and they are enjoying similar prosperity. A handful of them deserve special attention—one has a large population, one a small, and two are medium-sized. I'll begin with the one I've never visited. North Dakota is not exactly a mecca for tourists, but I'd love to see it now. The future of America's energy industry and its job-generating power are on display there.

Just as an energy boom lifted populous Texas to economic success on a global scale, so North Dakota, sprawling across the northern edge of the Great Plains border with Saskatchewan and Manitoba, with a population only slightly larger than El Paso's, is raising eyebrows and teaching lessons. While Texas had the second-fastest economic growth in the country in 2013, North Dakota claimed the top spot. Its exploding economy grew five times faster than the national average.[1]

That was North Dakota's third year in first place in the Bureau of Economic Analysis rankings. The reason is simple: the state sits atop an enormous amount of oil, and North Dakotans are not afraid to go get it. The Bakken formation yields a million barrels a day and is the source of more than 10 percent of the nation's crude oil production. As in the Texas of over a century ago, oil exploration is attracting workers and creating boomtowns like Williston, which saw a one-year population jump of almost 10 percent. Two hours south, in Dickinson, similar growth has created a housing shortage (a problem the marketplace will surely address).

Ever hear someone refer to an unemployment rate of roughly 5 percent as the standard for "full employment"? That notion draws laughter in the capital city of Bismarck. The state's jobless rate in 2013 was below 3 percent—and falling. Oil production has created jobs and a rich tax base that finances the schools and roads made necessary by the waves of new workers.

North Dakota is the greatest beneficiary of the "Drill, baby, drill!" ethic so despised by environmental zealots. But North Dakota is doing exactly what needs to be done to achieve what large majorities of Americans say they want—energy independence.

Do we even appreciate what that means anymore? After years of hearing the term from the lips of Democrats who long to go off fossil fuels cold turkey in favor of inconsistent renewables, North Dakota is joining Texas to show the nation and the world what it really takes to wean ourselves from oil imported from hostile countries: oil found beneath our own soil and off our own shorelines.

The new breed of North Dakota wildcatter shares an entrepreneurial fire with the Texans of old, but oil exploration today requires high technology, artful negotiation, and big money changing hands before some wells are even struck. In neighboring Minnesota, the *Minneapolis Star-Tribune* published a series on the changes happening next door. The cast of characters featured grizzled natives and new arrivals looking for changed lives, including Vern Stiller, a middleman who works deals between oil companies and ranchers: "I drive around, smoke cigarettes, drink coffee, talk smart and write checks."[2]

Ranchers enjoy the income, oil companies enjoy the prospect of extended production and profit, and the state enjoys an influx of money and business it would not otherwise see. The value of domestic energy production is so self-evident that even the state's Democrats embrace it—against a national party that works to hinder it at every turn. Longtime senators Byron Dorgan and Kent Conrad were advocates of drilling our way to energy independence, as is the state's newest Democrat senator, Heidi Heitkamp, who joins her Republican colleague John Hoeven in favoring the Keystone XL pipeline.

It is amazing to see what happens when politicians break free from the iron grip of party leadership and focus on what is truly best for the public. Senator Heitkamp knows, and says often, that the Keystone XL project will bring even greater benefits to her state and, more notably, to the entire nation. And she does not stop there. Asked on the campaign trail in 2012 what she would say to President Obama about his energy policy, she told a forum in Bismarck, "I think the first thing that I say to the president is, 'You're wrong. You're wrong on energy. You're headed in the wrong direction. You made bad decisions. It is time for you to change your secretary of energy. It is time for you to get in the real world and give predictability.'"[3]

If the Northeast tends to elect liberal Republicans, North Dakota has offered up a rare breed of late, the center-left Democrat. Prior to the 2010 election, both of its U.S. senators and its lone congressman were Democrats. Heitkamp's Republican opponent, Congressman Rick Berg, tried to hang Obamacare around her neck and argued that North Dakota should help turn the Senate Republican so that the anti-drilling Harry Reid would no longer be majority leader. But Heitkamp had so effectively communicated her commitment to helping North Dakota remain an energy-production leader that a state with overwhelming GOP registration elected her anyway. There is no reason for the obstruction of domestic energy to be a plank in the Democratic platform. In the states where lives are made better, and our nation made safer, by oil and gas exploration, voters reward support for that contribution to our energy independence in a bipartisan fashion.

On the national stage, leadership from energy-rich states can teach a valuable lesson about the folly of shackling domestic production. The states breaking free of fossil fuel phobia will enjoy prosperity while giving the nation a better shot at true independence from foreign oil.

It has been said that North Dakota is our least-visited state. Other sparsely populated states such as Wyoming and South Dakota have big tourist attractions—Yellowstone, Mount Rushmore—that draw visitors. North Dakota, not so much. What the North Dakotans do have to offer is their shining example of how to embrace the gift of natural resources and put them to best use for people. While it may be our least-visited state, North Dakota deserves to be among our most appreciated.

CHAPTER TWENTY-NINE

PENNSYLVANIA

Not every oil and gas boom has to happen in a thinly populated state with few other major industries. Natural gas, for example, is powering a renewal of the economy in Pennsylvania, home of the big cities of Philadelphia and Pittsburgh, industries like coal and steel, and plenty of high-tech and service companies. It's one of America's more diverse business landscapes.

The power of gas is raising the Keystone State to the upper echelons of energy production. In 2013 it was tied with Alaska and Louisiana for second place (behind Texas) in natural gas production. Kent Moors, an expert on oil and gas policy at Duquesne University, told the *Pittsburgh Tribune-Review*, "Forget about natural gas being a bridge fuel.... [It] is a major component of the national energy balance going forward—no end in sight."[1]

Pennsylvania thus joins Texas, North Dakota, Louisiana, Wyoming, Oklahoma, and Colorado in the circle of states whose leaders appreciate the magnitude of the benefits that the new oil and gas boom can bestow. Governor Tom Corbett, a first-term Republican seeking reelection in 2014, faces a decision that every gas-rich state confronts: whether to put a tax on all of that gas yield. North Dakota is not shy about taxing its oil and natural gas harvests; that state has put more than a billion dollars in a savings account they will surely need to absorb the growth gas brings.[2] But Governor Corbett is resisting a field of Democrats pushing for a drilling tax, arguing that such a levy would drive the industry and its valuable jobs to other states.[3] That is a reasonable concern in a region where the Marcellus Shale formation spreads across Pennsylvania, New York, Ohio, Maryland, and West Virginia.

At least one of those states, however, is paralyzed in its energy policy, leaning away from taking advantage of the natural gas it is fortunate to possess. It's easy to guess which state that is—our old friend New York.

After more than five years of a drilling moratorium, Empire State energy companies are giving up and looking for friendlier partners. Chesapeake Energy walked away from thousands of acres of New York leases in the summer of 2013 when landowners and local governments tossed up too many obstacles to make the project worthwhile.

Ken Silverstein, writing at EnergyBiz.com, suggested that frackophobic New Yorkers should consider what's going on in nearby states that have found the safety concerns to be a mirage and that are now reaping the economic benefits. "Perhaps the best thing is to watch those Marcellus-based states that are currently drilling," he wrote, "allowing them to become national case studies as to whether the shale gas boom is both environmentally and economically beneficial." He concludes that with more evidence of success, "Pennsylvania could motivate New York to get off the fence."[4]

And as 2014 began, Governor Andrew Cuomo of New York pledged to make a decision on the moratorium before facing voters for reelection in November. On one side, he faces the voters in his base, many supporting a "frack-free New York." On the other, he faces a growing mountain of evidence that the moratorium was a dumb idea. In one of his last news conferences of 2013, he struck a cautious tone: "It's one of the most important decisions I think we will make as a government, with far-reaching consequences. It's more important to be right than fast." It remains to be seen if Cuomo is right in his decision, but no one needs to worry about his being fast.

If Cuomo wants to huddle with a fellow Democrat to compare notes, he should call Pennsylvania's own Ed Rendell, who served two terms as governor prior to Corbett. A former chairman of the Democratic National Committee, Rendell is a product of the East Coast liberal establishment, but he followed an independent course when he decided to open the Marcellus Shale to drilling when he was governor.

Rendell recognized that Marcellus promised a "gold rush" for a state that could use a boost. The next question was whether to tax it. Next-door neighbor West Virginia does, and Joe Manchin, the Democratic governor at the time, told Rendell to go for it. Taxation was not hindering drilling in West Virginia, and Manchin's administration was reaping the benefits and applying them to sorely needed services in a cash-strapped time.[5]

Republicans in the Pennsylvania General Assembly resisted the proposed tax and won, keeping Pennsylvania the only major state to produce natural gas but not to tax it. In the 2014 state election, the debate over whether to glean revenue from the Pennsylvania natural gas boom will continue to churn, but no one of consequence will be arguing that the lucrative and beneficial explorations should stop.

Might Pennsylvania's happy experience with energy production nudge the state toward other commonsense conservative reforms? A second term for Corbett and a majority GOP legislature could help. Pennsylvania, however, might lean Republican in the state capitol while continuing to vote for Democratic presidential candidates. Even in George H. W. Bush's 1988 landslide victory over Michael Dukakis, the Republican margin in Pennsylvania was barely two points. Since then, Pennsylvania has opted for Clinton twice, backed both of George W. Bush's opponents, and voted for Obama twice. Optimists will note the Obama margin of victory was cut in half in 2012.

Before his rise to prominence as an advisor to Bill Clinton, James Carville worked on Bob Casey Sr.'s successful gubernatorial campaign in Pennsylvania in 1986. Referring to the urban centers at each end of the state and the more conservative population across its midsection, Carville famously gave rise to the description of Pennsylvania as "Philadelphia in the east, Pittsburgh in the west, and Alabama in the middle." That characterization suggested that savvy politicians would offer different messages to different parts of the state. But the wise use of natural gas is changing the state's political landscape. One day Pennsylvania may be cities at both ends, open country in between, and some Texas logic scattered throughout.

CHAPTER THIRTY

INDIANA

I met Mitch Daniels during Super Bowl week 2011 in Dallas. I'm sure he remembers none of our two minutes of conversation, because he was a man on a mission: shaking as many hands as possible in his role as the host governor of the following year's Super Bowl in Indianapolis.

To welcome him, North Texas had shipped in a few days of Indiana-style winter weather. When Super Bowl XLV was awarded to us in 2007, we had bested an Indianapolis proposal, promoting our bid with some Texas-style braggadocio that fans and media would far rather experience a Texas winter than the Hoosier variety. Little did we know that our Super Bowl week would be hit by snow, ice, and bitter cold that made the sprawling Metroplex a nightmare for visitors expecting our usual midwinter highs of about sixty degrees. In any case, the NFL was sufficiently impressed by the Indianapolis bid that they awarded the following year's game to Lucas Oil Stadium, just a few blocks from the state capitol in Indianapolis.

So there was Governor Daniels, in a denim shirt and ball cap, looking like a guy who had wandered into the media center looking for spare tickets. But any political junkies in the hall would have spotted him, mostly on account of the burst of presidential speculation in his second term.

The local story of the Super Bowl knocked some of the politics off my radio show for a few days. But the glow from the installation of a Republican-led House of Representatives was still strong. Just a few weeks earlier, I had returned from covering the swearing-in of the 112th Congress, with John Boehner taking the gavel from Nancy Pelosi. Conservative spirits were high. It seemed like America was starting to sour on the Obama agenda, and we occupied ourselves with the parlor game of choosing our 2012 nominee a year before the Iowa caucuses.

Daniels moved the buzz meter for good reasons. After serving as director of the Office of Management and Budget under George W. Bush, he brought to the Indiana governor's office fiscal policies that were more conservative than those of the White House in which he had served. When he wore his Super Bowl XLVI cap into the Dallas Sheraton ballroom, I made a point to tell him his name was already coming up as I tested listener passions for possible 2012 standard-bearers. Daniels had said just a few weeks earlier that he would make a presidential campaign decision by May, so I chose not to badger him in the first days of February.

Instead, I simply congratulated him on bringing several conservative reforms to Indiana at a time when the nation's eyes were peeled for leadership at the state level. Daniels had substantially cut the number of state employees and was taking on various other aspects of his state's financial challenges. His efforts had drawn the attention of David Leonhardt of the *New York Times*, whose article on the Indiana governor I had read just a few weeks earlier.

"Of all the Republicans talking about the deficit these days, Mitch Daniels, the governor of Indiana, has arguably the most credibility," Leonhardt wrote, describing how Daniels, unlike Congress, actually has the guts to cut the size of government while talking tax cuts.[1] I joked briefly with the governor about a conservative's getting good press from the *Times*. He said he was glad to see any focus on reforms in Indiana, praised what Rick Perry was doing in Texas, and excused himself to go on to his next opportunity to plug his state's Super Bowl—which incidentally wound up with better weather than ours.

Indiana is not as red as the crimson jerseys at IU in Bloomington, but it seems to be snapping awake from 2008, when its electoral votes went to Obama by one percentage point. Voters preferred Mitt Romney by more than ten points in 2012, as they also elected Republican congressman Mike Pence to succeed Daniels as governor.

That victory followed another burst of presidential speculation—about Pence. At the 2010 Values Voters Summit in Washington, he won a presidential preference straw poll in a field containing, among others, Sarah Palin. He did it with a speech that proclaimed, "I am a Christian, a conservative, and a Republican, in that order."[2]

Social conservatism is bonding with fiscal conservatism in Indiana, and observers wonder whether the state will lean red again in 2016. While it is showing a taste for Republican governors, its vacant U.S. Senate seat went to Democrat Joe Donnelly over Tea Party favorite Richard Mourdock in 2012. On the other hand, as 2014 dawned the legislature was weighing a proposed state constitutional amendment forbidding the recognition of gay marriage.

Like many states, Indiana has liberal and conservative constituencies pulling it in opposite directions. But with a Republican governor and legislature, the stage is set for further reforms, such as eliminating the property tax on business equipment. Indiana joined the list of right-to-work states in 2012 and clobbered neighboring Illinois in the *Forbes* 2013 rankings of "Best States for Business and Careers."[3] In areas like regulatory environment, business costs, and growth prospects, Indiana ranked sixteenth, compared with Illinois at thirty-eighth.

A continuing trend of cutting taxes while still finding the money for school and infrastructure spending has Indiana insiders wondering if the state's success might return Pence to the White House parlor talk—along with other governors enjoying the happy results from doing what Republicans say they want to do nationally. As Mitch Daniels enjoys his second year as president of Purdue University, his successor is keeping Indiana focused on embracing the promise of limited government and lower tax burdens.

CHAPTER THIRTY-ONE

NORTH CAROLINA

The *Washington Post* headline from May 2013 nearly quivers with alarm: "In North Carolina, Unimpeded GOP Drives State Hard to the Right." I do not recall a *Post* headline circa 2009 describing an "unimpeded" Democrat party driving America "hard to the left," even though that's exactly what they were and exactly what they did. Even with a Republican House since 2011, that push continues, while evidence of the resulting damage mounts.

In North Carolina, fortunately, a new Republican governor is joining with a GOP legislature to contradict the once-fashionable view of the Tar Heel State as the vanguard of the new South susceptible to the Obama mystique. Unlike many of its Southern neighbors, North Carolina has never had a long stretch of uniformly conservative leadership. In the U.S. Senate, the state that gave us the archetypal conservative Jesse Helms has also given us Sam Ervin, John Edwards, and Kay Hagan. As for the new Republican governor, Pat McCrory, he is only the third GOP governor since the nineteenth century. It has been nearly 150 years since a Republican governor of North Carolina has had a Republican General Assembly to work with.

The *Post* article enumerates various reforms under way that would match the agenda of any conservative Texan: drug testing for welfare recipients, voter ID, and resistance to Medicaid expansion and other aspects of Obamacare. They're even seeking to cut jobless benefits on the theory that if you subsidize something, you get more of it, including unemployment.

But the most important point of convergence is taxes. State senator Phil Berger explains, "North Carolina is a high income tax state, and we're suffering the consequences.... Our high tax rates are hindering economic growth and pushing jobs to our neighbors."[1] North Carolina Republicans are seriously trying to eliminate the state income tax. Number crunchers say the state might have to increase its sales tax by extending it to groceries and prescription drugs, but there's room for that. The sales tax in most counties is 6.25 percent, 2 percent less than in Texas, where we exempt food and medicine. That's a lot of wiggle room. Texas's sales tax is comparatively high, but the absence of an income tax seems to be a powerful draw for people and business. There's a lesson there for North Carolina as it ponders an income-tax-free future.

If conservative progress is measured by the degree of panic on the Left, North Carolina is advancing admirably. For the state's Democrats, the street dances of 2008 must seem like a generation ago. Out of 4.3 million votes cast in North Carolina that year,

Barack Obama beat John McCain by about 14,000, or 0.3 percent. In 2012, Romney won by 2 percent—enough to undermine the narrative that the state might be purple, trending blue. In July 2013, MSNBC's Rachel Maddow was driven to mock the reforms in North Carolina as "conservatives gone wild." One can only hope.

Any time grown-ups take control and shut down the romper rooms of the Left, there will be howling. But in North Carolina, vanquished liberals have been particularly unruly. In a protest movement with the curious moniker "Moral Mondays," citizens unhappy with the state's new direction file into the state capitol in Raleigh as each week begins with the express purpose of being arrested. Police have obliged, arresting nearly a thousand of them in 2013. While "Moral Mondays" sounds like a pastime for cranks with too much time on their hands, the carnival spread to Georgia in early 2014, where protesters were livid over Republican governor Nathan Deal's decision to decline federal funds for Medicaid expansion under Obamacare.

The angry reaction reflects the boldness of the initiatives in North Carolina and other states that are taking a hard look at liberal policies with a record of failure. The stunner has been Wisconsin, a solidly blue state that elected a Republican governor, Scott Walker, and a Republican U.S. senator, Ron Johnson, in 2010. Unfortunately, the Badger State swung back to the left in 2012, sending to the Senate the ultraliberal Tammy Baldwin, who trounced Republican Tommy Thompson, the longest-serving governor in the history of the state.

If North Carolina takes a conservative course, it might be able to rival the business climate of South Carolina, whose citizens make BMWs and Boeing fuselage systems. A key measure of

North Carolina's political temperature will come in the 2014 Senate elections as first-term Democrat Kay Hagan faces reelection in a political climate very different from 2008, when the Obama surge swept her to victory over the incumbent, Republican Elizabeth Dole. Her positions on most economic and social issues would make her right at home in New York or California, so her electoral fate will reveal how serious North Carolinians are about following Texas's path to prosperity.

Governor McCrory won't face voters again until 2016. If his constituents embrace his conservative reforms, he may find himself mentioned as a possible running mate for the Republican presidential nominee. Turning New York and California around may require changes on a revolutionary scale. But from the Carolinas to the Dakotas and in transitional states like Pennsylvania, Indiana, and Wisconsin, the values and principles that have made Texas so maddeningly successful are starting to spread, and with them, the hope that our nation can recover from the ravages of liberalism through shared sacrifice, equality of opportunity, and fiscal discipline.

PART VII

LONE STAR LUMINARIES

GOVERNOR RICK PERRY

When the *New York Times* praised Governor Rick Perry for juvenile justice reforms in 2011, no one should have expected it to become a habit. The editorial page editor of the nation's "newspaper of record" can't stand him. For proof, look at the July 8, 2013, blog piece by Andrew Rosenthal, who took time out from sifting through reader mail that day to ridicule Perry on the occasion of his announcement not to seek a fourth term.[1] "A consistent source of comic relief," the editor called him, lampoonable not just because of the infamous "oops" on a presidential debate stage—the moment when he could not recall the third agency he would abolish as president—but because of his pro-life stance ("a systematic assault on reproductive health services" as he "starved Planned Parenthood of money"). And Perry, Rosenthal reports with horror, was one of a "gang of Republican governors who refused to open a health exchange in accordance with the Affordable Care Act."

No doubt about it, James Richard Perry, who became governor on December 21, 2000, has often seemed to exist to annoy the Left—which is why he has wielded such power in Texas and why he excited so much presidential buzz in 2011. That buzz, of course, didn't last. Though the national media and Texas liberals attribute the crash landing of Perry's 2012 presidential campaign to his manifest unworthiness for higher office, I keep telling people that underestimating him is a big mistake. As 2016 draws near, Rick Perry brings a package that would have instant impact again—and this time he would be less likely to falter. I am not predicting that he will be the 2016 nominee. I am merely observing that those who doubt his credentials forget two things—America's short attention span and its likely taste in 2016 for scrappy conservative governors.

When I first met Rick Perry in 1994, he had been a Republican for only five years. In his six years in the state legislature, he had been one of a breed rarely found today—a Democrat willing to reduce spending. Backing Al Gore in the 1988 primaries (which eventually yielded Michael Dukakis as the nominee) was the last Democrat-flavored thing Perry did.

Our first interview was on the campaign trail as he sought a second term as the Texas agriculture commissioner. Our conversations were centered on marketing Texas crops to other states and other nations. Those talks broadened in 1998 as he sought the lieutenant governor's office being vacated by Democrat Bob Bullock, who got along famously with Governor George W. Bush. The era of fairly conservative Democrats holding statewide office in Texas was drawing to a close. Perry won narrowly and settled in for a brief ride as "Lite Guv," as the office is known, an ironic colloquialism since the lieutenant governor of Texas has more legislative clout than the governor.

The world knew Perry could soon move into the governor's mansion, because it was obvious George W. Bush would start planning a 2000 presidential run on the drive home from his second inaugural ball in Austin. Perry was a perfect fit in a state that had gone solid red. More conservative than Bush and less interested in the veneer of bipartisanship, he launched what became a fourteen-year agenda of fiscal and social conservatism that has earned the praise of many Republicans and the scorn of many Democrats.

His first actual election as governor came in a 2002 cakewalk against oil and gas developer Tony Sanchez. But four years later, he faced a trio of challengers who made for an odd dance, even by Texas standards. No incumbent who is a heavy favorite wants to spend a lot of time talking about his competition, but the field was filled with such a cast of characters that there was no avoiding it. Carole Keeton Strayhorn ran as "One Tough Grandma," a slogan she had used successfully in her race for state comptroller in 1998. Rather than lose in a Republican primary that might have lured U.S. senator Kay Bailey Hutchison, she chose to run as an independent and a moderate alternative to Perry.

She was not the only colorful independent in the mix. When the songwriter, philosopher, and humorist Kinky Friedman threw his familiar black hat into the ring, we knew we were in for a combination of high comedy and high drama. The author of the country song "They Ain't Makin' Jews Like Jesus Anymore," Friedman shared with my radio audience his unique "Five Mexican Generals Plan" for ending illegal immigration. He would divide the border into five regions, placing a Mexican general in charge of each. Two million dollars would be placed in an account for each general. Five thousand dollars would be withdrawn for each illegal immigrant crossing the border through that general's jurisdiction. "Problem solved," Kinky declared proudly, "and for only ten million."

In the jostle for front-of-mindedness, Strayhorn sought to appear on the ballot as "Carole Keeton Grandma Strayhorn." She argued that since Friedman appeared as "Richard 'Kinky' Friedman," she should get "Grandma." It didn't fly; "Kinky" had been Friedman's actual professional name for decades.

There was a perfectly able Democrat on the ballot, a former congressman at that. But poor Chris Bell, a man of quality and substance, was the fourth-most-interesting candidate in the race, and he ultimately garnered just under 30 percent of the vote, mostly because of the "D" beside his name. Grandma and Kinky shared another 30 percent of the vote, leaving Perry with barely 39 percent. But it was still a nearly ten-point win, which anyone will take in a crowded field. The election of 2006 had been a weird ride, and Perry was happy to have it in his rear-view mirror.

Perry enjoyed calm seas through his first full term. But as his second term began, he stumbled into a controversy he did not see coming. He issued an executive order in February 2007 mandating a vaccine against human papillomavirus for girls entering the sixth grade.[2] The stated purpose was to prevent cervical cancer, to which HPV is linked.

The mandate's goal was noble, but the methodology sent Perry's conservative base into revolt. First, it bypassed the legislature. Callers lined up to ask, "If this was such a pressing need, why not address it through normal legislative channels?" But the notion of a government-mandated vaccine, especially when the need for it depends on sexual behavior, touched a conservative nerve. It didn't help that the vaccine, Gardasil, is a product of Merck & Co., whose Texas lobbyist had once been Perry's chief of staff.

I had several conversations with the governor about the controversy. He defended the executive order on the grounds of urgency, especially in a state whose legislature meets every other year. And though the vaccine was "compulsory," Perry pointed out that objecting parents could opt out on behalf of their daughters.

On my phone lines, no sale. Parents wanted to opt *in* rather than having to jump through even the slightest hoop to avoid a mandate from Austin. And the urgency argument went precisely nowhere. "There is no emergency other than in the boardrooms of Merck," said Dawn Richardson, president of Parents Requesting Open Vaccine Education.[3] The legislature that Perry sought to bypass for efficiency's sake was more than efficient in passing a bill to undo his order. He relented, and eventually distanced himself from the entire matter, calling the order a "mistake."

After his third gubernatorial election in 2010, in which he easily parried a primary challenge from the popular Kay Bailey Hutchison, speculation turned to a presidential run. Perry entered the race in August 2011, later than most but with high expectations. The campaign, however, did not pan out as many had hoped. A nearly unperturbed decade as governor of the nation's most successful state made Perry a formidable candidate on paper, but he soon learned that the national arena could be considerably more hazardous than the friendly confines of Texas.

As soon as he entered the race, Perry became a big target. His Republican opponents attacked him for referring to Social Security (accurately enough) as a "Ponzi scheme," and Michele Bachmann tried, with little success, to make an issue out of the HPV vaccine controversy.

With the Iowa caucuses still more than three months away, the calendar was peppered with debates across the nation. In his second debate, Perry was the punching bag for the Gardasil initiative. The third, ten days later, featured another self-detonated bomb, the now-infamous "I don't think you have a heart," leveled at those who disagreed with him about the education of the children of illegal immigrants. This was such a needless flap. No one had suggested barring those children from schools; the only issue was whether they should be granted in-state tuition rates. Nonetheless, Perry took heat from a large contingent that felt he had maligned all advocates of tough immigration laws.

Speaking to a friendly audience in New Hampshire on October 28, Perry was relaxed and loose, perhaps to a degree the national media had not seen. When the eight-minute edit of a twenty-five-minute speech hit YouTube, an amused chorus suggested he must have been drinking. When I watched the video, I recognized Perry in his rambling and folksy mode—something that would not raise an eyebrow among those who know him. But to those who didn't, and especially the political opponents among them, it was a field day that extended to the very next *Saturday Night Live*, featuring Bill Hader as Perry, explaining that rival candidate and pizza mogul Herman Cain had offered him a curious pie: "I realized the pepperonis were Ambien and the tomato sauce was beer."

Funny stuff, but probably not at Perry campaign headquarters. The caucuses were still two months away, which could have been plenty of time to right the ship. Except that an iceberg lay dead ahead, and it was floating in Perry's own brain.

He was on a roll on November 9 in a CNBC debate focusing on economic issues, making one of those bottom-line observations that make the Frank Luntz focus groups turn their dials in an approving direction: "I think we're getting all tangled up around an issue here about 'Can you work with Democrats' or 'Can you work with Republicans.' Yeah, we can all do that. But the fact of the matter is that we'd better have a plan in place that Americans can get their hands around, and that's the reason my flat tax is the only one of all the folks, these good folks on the stage—it balances the budget in 2020, it does the things to the regulatory climate that has to happen."

Except for subject-verb agreement, this was solid stuff: hitting big themes, addressing his competitors as well as the audience with good eye contact and authoritative gestures—the kind of natural comfort you cannot teach.

And then, the sickening jolt as Perry collided with the iceberg. If only he had ended his answer with the remark about the regulatory climate. But no, he had other small-government points to squeeze into his remaining seconds. What about those three agencies he would flat-out eliminate as soon as he took Oval Office?

Turning to Ron Paul on his left, Perry held out his hand to count them off. "I will tell you, it's three agencies of government, when I get there, that are gone." I love this kind of talk, and I felt the audience was loving it too.

"Commerce"—up went his thumb. "Education"—out went the index finger.

The third finger shot out, but the accompanying answer did not. He touched his left temple. "What's the third one there, let's see…." There was a smattering of laughter, mostly nervous. Paul egged him on by suggesting that *five* agencies should be eliminated. The icy seawater rushed in through the long gash in the hull. "Commerce, Education, and, uh, the, uh—." From the end of the stage, a helpful suggestion from Mitt Romney: "EPA?" Desperate for a lifeboat, Perry leapt in: "EPA, there you go," but he shook his head smiling, knowing that wasn't it.

"Seriously?" asked panelist John Harwood. "Is the EPA the one you were talking about?"

I yelled at my TV screen: "Energy! Energy! You're the governor of *Texas*! Of course it's Energy!"

He did not hear me. Meanwhile, Harwood had to know history was being made. "You can't name the third one?"

"The third agency of government I would—I would do away with the Education, uh, the, uh, Commerce, and let's see.... I can't. The third. Sorry." And we're done.

"Oops."

I died a little inside. Apparently more than Perry did. He was positively nonchalant in recalling that night later, figuring it was just one of those things. He later attributed his generally spotty performances to back surgery he had undergone in June 2011, which he says left him unable to log his daily runs and thus unable to sleep well.

In the days following, Perry sought refuge in self-deprecating humor. The damage was done, but Perry was not. Knowing that public attention would evanesce as the holidays approached, he front-loaded the month of December with the campaign video called "Strong."

It was strong, all right. A strong outreach to the people Perry would need to pull him out of the wreckage. Strolling in a wooded setting, he addresses the camera: "I'm not ashamed to admit that

I'm a Christian. But you don't need to be in the pew every Sunday to know that there's something wrong in this country when gays can serve openly in the military, but our kids can't openly celebrate Christmas or pray in school."

Wow. Three hot buttons hit in eighteen words over about five seconds. Possibly a record.

"As president, I'll end Obama's war on religion, and I'll fight against liberal attacks on our religious heritage," he continues. Then the capper: "Faith made America strong; it can make her strong again."

Then the legally required: "I'm Rick Perry, and I approve this message."

And I did too. I approved of it mightily. Within the construct of appealing to the conservative base needed to win the nomination, there was no one else who was willing to connect this directly with conservatives' grievances about a secular-progressive president.

It was not an attack on gays, as the Left predictably cried, but a juxtaposition of what is permissible and what is impermissible in Obama's America. Highlighting that contrast could have been a springboard back into the front lines of the 2012 race. But time was short as the campaigns went into the holiday deep freeze, and the Iowa caucuses loomed just three days into the new year.

Time was short but obstacles were many. Mitt Romney was spending imposing amounts of money, and Rick Santorum was spending imposing amounts of time, visiting every one of Iowa's ninety-nine counties.

On caucus eve, I drove from Des Moines forty miles northwest through farmland bathed in a setting sun. I was to emcee the last Rick Perry rally, which was held in Perry, Iowa, a nice touch by a campaign that had to know its hours were dwindling. On hand to show the governor some love were country star Larry Gatlin and neighboring governor Bobby Jindal of Louisiana. Gatlin knocked out three acoustic numbers as the crowd gathered in the small, historic Hotel Pattee. Among the campaign buttons on sale in the lobby, a masterpiece: it said "Oops" in large letters with the first "O" the familiar logo of Barack Obama. I had introduced Jindal at Perry events in Texas before. Their friendship is real, and so was the affection he expressed in support of the candidate, who spoke briefly but energetically about the need to finish strongly the next day.

He finished fifth, behind Santorum, Romney, Paul, and Newt Gingrich. Romney was erroneously declared the winner that night, but there was no mistaking 12,557 votes cast for Perry, compared with Santorum's and Romney's nearly thirty thousand apiece or Ron Paul's twenty-six thousand. The Perry campaign was effectively over. Mitt Romney smoked the field the following week in New Hampshire, as Perry collected less than 1 percent of the vote. On January 19, Perry exited the race and endorsed Gingrich.

In our next conversation, I asked why the endorsement for a candidate whom I had always said would never be our party's nominee. (I have enormous admiration for Newt, but that did not affect my objective view of his chances. His strengths are intelligence and courage. A campaign requires a slavish devotion to a series of easily digestible messages, a regimen he will never warm to. I hope Newt knows this is a compliment.)

There was no way Perry was going to endorse Romney. He was cordial with Santorum, but ultimately went with the sharper edges of Gingrich, who had written the foreword to Perry's book *Fed Up! Our Fight to Save America from Washington.*

"Oops" is ancient history. Today, the attention of journalists, pundits, and pollsters is fixed on 2016. Governors like New Jersey's Chris Christie (and Louisiana's Jindal and Wisconsin's Scott Walker) are a hot commodity because they have run states and guided an executive branch and achieved identifiable conservative reforms.

Governor Perry will leave the governor's mansion in January 2015. Except for seven days in 1991, between leaving House District 64 and taking the oath as agriculture commissioner, he will have spent thirty years in continuous office. He is a rare example of a longtime politician who can still get a roar from a Tea Party crowd. That talent cannot be ignored as 2016 draws near. Other names have occupied more headlines since 2012, but no one can match his record of fighting the Obama agenda from the encampment of a state that has marched through these punishing times not just surviving but thriving.

Anyone who thought Perry was a spent political cartridge was in for a surprise at the 2014 Conservative Political Action Conference in Washington. As bleary-eyed attendees settled in for the first day of speeches after a night of conservative merrymaking, out strode Perry to the strains of AC/DC's "Back in Black." "Let's go! Come on! Get it up!" he exhorted—not exactly the opening you'd get in a McCain or Romney speech.

Which is a vital point. It's not what CPAC heard from any other speakers, who represented a wide range of ages, backgrounds, and ideological passion. The man who gave us the "oops" moment in 2012 is the same guy who delivered the signature line of CPAC 2014: "It's time for a little rebellion on the battlefield of ideas." He brought the crowd to its feet for the longest sustained in-speech applause of the convention. He did it with a common-man directness that will serve any 2016 hopeful well.

Perry spread a rhetorical banquet before an audience hungering for effective conservative leadership: "It is time for Washington to focus on the few things the Constitution establishes as the federal government's role: Defend our country! Provide a cogent foreign policy! And what the heck—deliver the mail, preferably on time, and on Saturday!"

Then, with the swagger that comes out when he knows he's connecting, "Get out of the healthcare business! Get out of the education business! Stop hammering industry! Let the sleeping giant of American enterprise create prosperity again!" By this point the applause was deafening, but there was no drowning out his rousing peroration: "My fellow conservatives! The future of this nation is upon you! It belongs to you! *You* have the power to change America! *You* have the power to speak to our newest hopes in addition to our age-old dreams! *You* are the path to the future, a light on a distant shore. And *you* represent the renewed hope that America can be great again!"

Chris Christie may be the master of relating to an audience on a regular-guy level. But for those weary of counting the holes in the New Jersey governor's swiss-cheese conservatism, Perry's applause-drenched passion at CPAC was a far better measure of the man than a few clumsy seconds on a dog-and-pony debate stage in 2011.

The 2016 race will begin the day after the 2014 votes are in. Among the possible Republican contenders to restore what's left of the country when *Marine One* carries Barack Obama away from the White House on that blessed January 20 of 2017, none arouses more interest and passion than Perry's fellow Texan Ted Cruz. As the nation asks how far yet another Texan may go, the possible answers begin with where he came from.

CHAPTER THIRTY-THREE

SENATOR TED CRUZ

Before I ever met Ted Cruz, I met his father.

On April 15, 2009, three queasy months into the Age of Obama, the Tea Party was taking shape with rallies across America. Local Dallas organizers were kind enough to ask me to serve as emcee for our city's event that afternoon in front of City Hall.

The charm of the Tea Party has always been that it does not run on an engine of big names, big money, or big Washington influence, maintaining a healthy skepticism of all three. So as a list of local entrenched politicians asked for microphone time and were politely declined, the agenda took shape. I introduced an inspiring line of activists, constitutionalists, conservative organizers, and private citizens, all fed up with the big-government status quo. We were looking to wrap the event at dusk, which was drawing near.

Then I was asked about welcoming an added speaker, a gentleman who was available to share his story of escaping from Cuba on the eve of Castro's conquest. Compelling stuff, but we were running a little late as it was, and I thought about respectfully resisting a late addition, a good idea when agendas start to get loose and long and you start to lose the room.

It was their call, not mine, but as I looked out over a crowd that had not lost a speck of energy after a long schedule of speakers, I thought, "What the heck? The more the merrier." And I met Rafael Cruz. I suggested that with darkness falling, he should keep it within three to five minutes. He went easily twenty, and left us wanting more. "Communism does not work!" he repeated, sharing stories of how he had seen it unfold in his native land and how he sees its building blocks rising higher in his chosen American homeland under Obama.

Over the top? Not for this crowd. The applause for Mr. Cruz echoed as attendees disbanded, energized for the long term, knowing it would take Herculean efforts to dig out of a spending hole dug deep by presidents and Congresses of both parties.

As the Tea Party spread its wings and looked toward striking blows for liberty and sane government in 2010, Rafael Bienvenido Cruz's son, Rafael Edward (Ted) Cruz, was pondering a run for Texas attorney general to succeed Greg Abbott, who had appointed him to the post of solicitor general in 2003 and was considering a run for governor. But Abbott eventually decided to run for reelection as attorney general, so Cruz focused on private-sector work with his Houston law firm until January of 2011, when he announced his quest for the U.S. Senate seat of the retiring Kay Bailey Hutchison.

This vacancy attracted a crowded field, pitting Cruz against the sitting lieutenant governor, David Dewhurst, who was basking in the glow of the Texas Miracle. Other rivals included the smart and talented mayor of Dallas, Tom Leppert, and Craig James, an ESPN commentator and 1980s SMU football star. Dewhurst led the field by ten points in the primary election, on May 29, 2012, but at 44 percent he was short of the majority needed to avoid a runoff. Cruz came in second at 34 percent.

Runoffs are about how many voters the top finisher can lure back a second time. Dewhurst faced a dual challenge: two more months of campaigning, and facing Cruz, a human buzz saw, one-on-one. Two stories dominated the weeks leading up to the July 31 election—the snowballing strength of the Cruz phenomenon and the self-destruction of Dewhurst.

David Dewhurst is a man of character and substance, an admirable conservative who deserves his share of credit for maintaining Texas's prosperity through tough times. But in the contest against Cruz, his campaign made some fatal miscalculations. He seems to have assumed that the 56 percent of Republicans who voted against him in the primary would be automatically inclined to support his opponent in the runoff. In the face of such odds, his campaign went negative—viciously so. Dewhurst's ads tried to connect Cruz, through his law firm, to various unsavory business ventures, but the obvious overreaching backfired, and Cruz won the runoff easily—57 to 43 percent.

However ill advised Dewhurst's strategy was, it's hard to say what else might have worked. It was Cruz's moment. He perfectly captured the mood of the voters, rocketing past one of the familiar stars of Texas politics and into an entirely new galaxy of

expectations. It was an ascendency like few others in recent memory, reminiscent, ironically, of Barack Obama's.

For his part, Dewhurst faced another challenge from the
right, from state senator Dan Patrick, and lost the 2014 primary
for lieutenant governor on March 27.

Could Cruz live up to the hype? His first year in office showed
that if there was anything more compelling than Cruz the candidate, it was Cruz the actual senator. On issues from Obamacare
to federal spending to Second Amendment rights to protecting
the unborn, he has shown everyone how to energize a conservative
Republican base. He has infuriated the Left and invigorated the
Right. There is simply no one like him in the Senate, or maybe
anywhere else. Senator Cruz has been a frequent and enthusiastic
guest on my North Texas talk show, and his eagerness to connect
with his constituents is a valuable lesson about political clout these
days. Doing talk radio often and well is not necessary for success
in conservative politics, but there is no platform quite like it.

Local talk shows and even many nationally syndicated shows
could not get Mitt Romney to spare five precious minutes as he
crisscrossed the nation in 2012 trying to make the case that the
people should make him their president. There is a risk in such
appearances for any candidate with shaky conservative street cred:
the occasional host may ask a challenging question or two. But
once Romney was the nominee, even lukewarm hosts would have
joined a broadcast army to help him return Barack Obama to
private life. But that wasn't his priority. That's not why he lost, but
it's part of the reason Mitt Romney will be remembered as a candidate who couldn't connect with the grassroots.

Ted Cruz, by comparison, is a connectivity machine. His
operation knows local and national radio and TV people in every

time zone by first name. During his seemingly quixotic fight to defund Obamacare—a fight that led to the government shutdown in 2013—I wondered if I might see him dismantling the Affordable Care Act in the kitchen with Rachael Ray one day. He was everywhere.

It may be too early for a verdict on the defunding fight. Admirers and detractors alike said he was attempting the impossible with the Senate and the White House controlled by Democrats. The effort eventually fell short. Everyone—the Republican establishment, the media, certainly the Democrats—said it was a foolish stunt by a political showman who doesn't know how to choose his battles. The boy wonder from Texas, they said, whose star had shone so bright in 2010, had given himself two black eyes.

Cruz himself was not disheartened, drawing strength from his millions of supporters. In their eyes, he was an American version of "Tank Man," the still-unidentified figure who stood on Changan Avenue along Tiananmen Square in Beijing in 1989, blocking tanks just after the Chinese military had killed hundreds if not thousands of protesters.

Nevertheless, nearly everyone except the Tea Party considered Cruz's gambit a disaster. The GOP took a dive in the polls, and President Obama looked whip-smart by comparison. Then came the disastrous rollout of Obamacare in November and the first wave of health insurance cancellations. Suddenly the playing field was tilted back in Cruz's direction in a lightning-fast and soul-satisfying reversal of public opinion.

The spirit of rebellion was alive again. Texas Republicans who had rarely come under fire found themselves facing the prospect and in some cases the reality of challenges from the Right. Their opponents echoed Cruz's battle cry: This is no time for faint hearts or half measures. Our liberty is in danger, and time to save our nation is running out. This message is attracting a wide, strong fan base among Texas conservative voters. Not that every Cruz-lite challenger can succeed against long-standing incumbents, but the playing field has been re-striped.

If Ted Cruz runs for president, how will his act play on a national stage? It can be argued it is already on a national stage, as he has traveled through many states campaigning for people and causes he believes in. No one in Congress has received as much attention since the 2012 election. No freshman senator in history has been this big a deal. Cruz was a finalist for *Time* magazine's 2013 Person of the Year. If we had not installed a new pope in March, he may well have snagged its designation as the figure of greatest impact in the year's news. A Rasmussen poll at the end of 2013 found only Pope Francis and President Obama ahead of Cruz for most influential person *in the world*.[1]

But let's tap the brakes for a moment. No doubt about it, Cruz is a phenomenon without any recent parallel. The 2016 field is made up of precisely one other person with as forceful a demeanor, and that's New Jersey governor Chris Christie, who comes with a steamer trunk filled with mixed ideological baggage and a reputation smudged by Bridgegate. There are noble and talented conservatives available, but none with Cruz's talent for firing up the base.

It is easy to see him capturing the 2016 nomination, but an actual campaign has to play out first. How would that go? Who would the main challengers be? What would be the inevitable unforeseen surprises that are always there to lift some candidates from obscurity or knock others from a high perch?

And the ultimate question: If he were the nominee, how would he do in a general election, especially against Hillary Clinton? By

November 2016, will America be so weary of eight years of Obama that they thirst for change as they did after four years of Carter? Would Hillary pose an insurmountable obstacle of yet more history to be made as millions try to bring about the first woman presidency?

Until the 2014 elections, Cruz will have to settle for a deliciously vague role as the most influential politician in America other than the president. If he decides to ride that role to higher altitudes, many corners of the nation will get additional doses of what we have seen in Texas for the last few years. A Cruz run would settle a question that has kept my talk show lines buzzing for years: What would happen if a bold, unapologetic conservative with razor-sharp debate skills actually won the nomination?

If Ted Cruz is conservatism's learned constitutional scholar of the moment, another Texas Ted brings passion on similar subjects but with a different set of tools.

CHAPTER THIRTY-FOUR

TED NUGENT

With all due respect for the leaders of the National Rifle Association and Gun Owners of America, there is just no match for the common-man clout of Ted Nugent, whose impact dates back nearly fifty years to his first weapons of choice, the Gibson Byrdland and other assorted guitars.

There are layers of genius in my favorite Nugentism, which I quoted earlier: "Guns don't kill people; gun-free zones kill people." It sets the listener up to expect the familiar ending, "people kill people." That well-known saying wisely underlines the fact that guns are inanimate objects made either beneficial or harmful by the hands holding them. But the head fake sets the reader up for Ted's own fresh insight—"gun-free zones kill people"—and starts a new debate, one that we desperately need to have today if we want to keep both our citizens and our Constitution safe.

For too long, gun haters have insisted that the public is safer when guns are denied to law-abiding people. The gun control lobby has been utterly undeterred by a thick book of tragic shootings that their pet policies would have done nothing to stop. From Aurora to Newtown to wherever tragedy may strike next, the gun grabbers can be counted on to recommend banning the very solution that can save lives—arming law-abiding citizens. What do school shooters, movie theater shooters—virtually all shooters everywhere—have at their disposal? A long list of venues where we have unwisely told good people with guns that they are not allowed to stop bad people with guns

So in the fight against this army of anti-firearms zealots, whom do you want walking point? Someone standing at a lectern in a thousand-dollar suit, or Ted in fatigues pointing out, "If guns cause crime, all of mine are defective"? This is not a slight to the good people (some in very nice suits) at the NRA, where Ted is a board member. I honor in particular Wayne LaPierre, who is now in his third decade as executive vice president of America's largest gun-rights organization. But Nugent is unique—to use a most misused word. People say "unique" when they mean only rare or uncommon, so you hear gaffes such as "Which of these is more unique?" As the word's root suggests, unique means there is only one.

There is only one Ted Nugent. And he is now a Texan.

Ted brings to the state not just a passion for gun rights, but a bullhorn in support of the entire Bill of Rights, which he views as under attack from not just Barack Obama but a long-toiling line of leftists he's had in his (metaphoric) sights for a long time. So what led Ted to pack up the family a decade ago and settle near Waco, forsaking the interior of Michigan, the state where he spent his childhood and most of his adult life?

I feel privileged to have heard the answer firsthand, as the result of a friendship of almost twenty years. You may have gathered that Ted is a hunter. He still says there is little to compare to brisk autumn bow hunting in his beloved Michigan. But by the 1990s, Ted had found lots of good hunting in Texas too—and lots of kindred spirits. He made frequent visits here, enjoying hunting, camaraderie, political conversations, and activism. At some point, he learned of a radio guy in Dallas–Fort Worth with a shared sense of liberty in distress. So he called me to tell me he appreciated what I was doing, and to offer to appear as a guest on my show.

I immediately flashed back twenty years to the middle of the 1970s. I was a mostly decent kid with mostly decent grades in high school, but my friends and I discovered beer a little too early, and I also discovered something else, which I love to this day—live music.

My eight-track collection embraced all of the great '70s artists—Elton John, Led Zeppelin, James Taylor, Billy Joel, Earth, Wind & Fire—and the creative arena bands of the day—Journey, Foreigner, Styx, and the like. The bottom line was that if I could scrape together the roughly ten dollars it took to see anyone from Zeppelin to the Who to Emerson, Lake and Palmer in those days, I was in.

So it was that I found myself with tickets for Black Sabbath on December 9, 1976, at the Capital Centre in Largo, Maryland. I had not been a voracious consumer of Ozzy and the boys, having only a lay teenager's familiarity with "Iron Man" and "Paranoid." But ever the student of the culture, I grabbed a copy of the just-released compilation, *We Sold Our Soul for Rock 'n' Roll,* and introduced myself to closet classics like "War Pigs" and "Fairies

Wear Boots." I also undertook some homework to get caught up on the opening act, Ted Nugent. I found much to enjoy in his just-released album, *Free-for-All*, so when the lights went down and the pot haze thickened, he launched into a set list I knew by heart. I had been barely familiar with Ted in his Amboy Dukes days in the late 1960s, when I was running at more of a Beatles and Motown speed. But as he tore through old material and new, finishing with ten sublime minutes of "Stranglehold," I was hooked for life.

Six months later, "Cat Scratch Fever" was eating up the charts, and two decades after that, he was on my cell phone.

Ted is the easiest interview anyone will ever conduct. Ask a question, enjoy three minutes of expertly woven "self-evident truth," ask the next question, repeat. We talked every few months, and not always about gun rights. He had a lot to say about the Clinton administration—he was not a fan—and he loved offering as a counterpoint his friend John Engler, Michigan's governor from 1991 to 2003, a Republican who had managed to win comfortably in a state with substantial labor constituencies and Democrat-heavy urban centers.

As his fiftieth birthday drew near during the Christmas season of 1998, my flip phone buzzed to life with "Uncle Ted" on the tiny screen. He was inviting me and my friend and technical producer, Sean Chastain, to his birthday gathering—just a houseful of friends at Rio Bonito Ranch outside Junction, in the heart of the beautiful Texas Hill Country.

We had known Ted for maybe two years, and we didn't know who the other attendees might be, but we figured we would not be rubbing elbows with Steven Tyler and ZZ Top. Ted's social circle ran more to veterans, hunters, and gun-rights activists, and those are the folks we looked forward to meeting as we rolled up the gravel road to the ranch's main house.

We gathered for a meal in Rio Bonito's common dining area, where Ted's birthday party guests mingled with other folks who just happened to be there that week to bass fish or hunt black buck antelope. But afterward, Ted's party settled in a living area, where friends who had known him for years made requests that he knocked out on an acoustic guitar in front of a roaring fire. He played "Hey Baby," "Great White Buffalo," even "Fred Bear," a tribute to a bow-hunting mentor—and I captured all of it on a clunky 1998-era video camera, which I lost somewhere between Rio Bonito and the Austin airport. I still wrestle with the bitterness.

But I came away with something that cannot be lost—a memory of hanging with Ted and his growing number of friends from Texas, a group whom he valued so much that he became their neighbor a few years later. He told me that night that Texas values resonated deeply with him; he felt he was Texan in every way but residentially. He fixed that by 2005, moving with his wife, Shemane, and son Rocco to a ranch down the road from George W. Bush in Crawford.

But that evening at Rio Bonito, after he sang a few songs and spoke of an urge to move to Texas, he stood up, thanked everyone, and went to bed. It was 8:45. He and his hunting brothers had been up since 4:00 a.m. and planned to get up at the same time the next morning. Not how Ozzy spent his fiftieth, I'm guessing.

Sean and I drove back to quiet Fredericksburg, Texas, and turned on the hotel TV to watch the C-SPAN replay of that day's Clinton impeachment debate in the House of Representatives.

This may be an odd birthday party story for a rock star, but it is vintage Ted. Visiting him backstage at a Dallas appearance years later, I saw tables stacked with water bottles and energy bars, the rooms shoulder to shoulder with hunting friends and veterans of wars from Vietnam to Iraq. This is his circle of blood brothers. The members of this community care about liberty, believe America is a force for good around the world, and have no patience with those who would trample our rights. I talk to Ted often, on and off the air, and the animated, unstoppable, uninterruptable, irrepressible character you get on radio and TV is no act.

At sixty-five, he still tours exhaustively. He does *everything* exhaustively, but he's never the one who seems exhausted. In the summer of 2006, he appeared at Billy Bob's Texas, the cavernous Fort Worth honky-tonk that broadens its spectrum at times to welcome the occasional Kansas or REO Speedwagon tour. On that hot Texas night, I enjoyed the privilege of introducing Ted to a throng of fans cut from the same cloth as his birthday party guest list—veterans, hunters, loud and proud middle-aged conservatives, sprinkled with folks of my era for whom "Cat Scratch" was a part of youth's soundtrack. As I yelled his name to bring him on, the band kicked into "Snakeskin Cowboys," which had been released as I entered my freshman year of college. Two hours later, after that extended solo from "Stranglehold," my wife and I and everyone else filed out, happy and drained. Ted may well have been back on his Texas property before I pulled into my driveway. "Why waste energy partying and rotting your mind with booze and drugs and poisons when we have a country to protect and liberty to defend?" he told me when I asked how he stayed clean in the drug-addled heyday of rock and roll.

★ ★ ★

As the 2014 Texas primary election and this book's final edit-
ing deadline drew near, Ted delivered a master class in why some
folks love him, why some folks hate him, and how he can sometimes make life tricky for those of us who call him a friend.

I'm sure it seemed like a great idea at Greg Abbott campaign
headquarters to have Uncle Ted on hand for a couple of stops as
the campaigning grew tedious and everyone was just waiting for
the March 4 election to get here. Abbott already owned the voting
bloc that resonates with Ted's issues of gun rights, strong borders,
and full-throated defense of the Constitution. But Ted brings
more energy to the campaign trail than anyone else alive.

Look out, though—if Ted's with you, reporters are going to
examine everything he has ever said about anyone—and that
includes some gonzo moments that go miles beyond the sharpest
talk show tongues or abrasive pundits.

Usually it is the kind of stuff dismissed as, "Well, that's Ted"—
wildly exaggerated between-song banter with adoring crowds on
a concert tour. But the comments that surfaced in February 2014,
from an interview at a gun show a month earlier, were harder to
dismiss. "I have obviously failed," Ted had lamented, "to galvanize
and prod, if not shame, enough Americans to be ever vigilant not
to let a Chicago Communist-raised, Communist-educated, Com-
munist-nurtured subhuman mongrel like the ACORN community
organizer gangster Barack Hussein Obama to weasel his way into
the top office of authority in the United States of America."

Not exactly a George Will excerpt from *Fox News Sunday*.
Facing a wave of radio callers wondering what I thought of my
buddy, I made clear that I wouldn't choose those words, but batted

away every charge that racism was on display. As CNN's Wolf Blitzer made a tortured connection between Ted's amped-up rhetoric and the Nazis' "Übermenschen" concept, and as every Ted hater within earshot lined up to say he knew his motivation was racial, all I could do was share years of experience with Ted and everyone who has ever known him.

As I explained, it is not Barack Obama's race that sends Ted over the edge, it is his politics. I urged doubters to look at his comments on black leaders like former Florida congressman Allen West and Supreme Court justice Clarence Thomas, and then try to suggest that Ted has a problem with black people. I am not aware of a white musician today who spends more time celebrating the African American roots of his craft than Ted.

Days later, Ted apologized—not so much to President Obama, but to Greg Abbott and any others he may show support for down the road. "I will try to elevate my vernacular to the level of those great men that I'm learning from in the world of politics."

★　★　★

Now a senior citizen "with a guitar and a middle finger," Ted spreads the gospel of eating what you kill, guarding your family and property with arms, and protecting your freedoms with all your heart. And along the way, as he wrote in *God, Guns, & Rock 'n' Roll*, "Kick maximum ass."

It's as if Ted and Texas were made for each other, each richer for the existence of the other. Once Ted is your friend, he is woven into the fabric of your life. I am proud to know him and blessed to call him a friend—and someday I'm sure my ears will stop ringing from that Billy Bob's gig.

PART VIII

CONCLUSION

CHAPTER THIRTY-FIVE

OUR LAST, BEST HOPE?

My friend Paul Gleiser of Tyler, Texas, doesn't just own radio station KTBB; he graces its airwaves and its website with a commentary called "You Tell Me," a series of observations on the issues of the day. His skill and insights evoke memories of another Paul—Paul Harvey, who spent nearly sixty years telling people what he thought and making it sound like the only way any reasonable person could possibly think.

On December 19, 2013, Paul delivered a commentary that strikes a chord with anyone who senses that this is the first era in American history when we will have to regret truly screwing things up for the next generation. His daughter, in her mid-twenties, faces struggles in life that are magnified by the bad decisions her parents' generation has made over the years: running up a crippling national debt, creating an entitlement-addicted underclass, and raising children who are bereft of historical and economic literacy and personal responsibility.

"We boomers simply cannot be forgiven for wasting all of the money," Paul said. "America's success in World War II and its resulting post-war economic dominance bequeathed to us national wealth on an unprecedented scale. That wealth is now gone and in its place stands a mountain of debt that my daughter and her peers will shoulder all the way to their graves."[1]

To return to doing right by our progeny, there are things we must do as a nation and things we must *stop* doing as a nation. America as we know it cannot long survive the spending binge we've been on for the past seventy years. Our children's welfare is jeopardized by a bankruptcy of culture, with countless kids spinning out of control because of insufficient parenting in a world replete with poisonous influences. The strong faith that once was the underpinning of the average American childhood is less prevalent. Our adults are less self-reliant, lured into inertia by an entitlement structure that rewards sloth and saps initiative and by a tax structure that punishes success.

Some of these problems can be addressed only at the national level. 2014 provides an opportunity to change the complexion of Congress, and 2016 offers the hope of a president who might actually have the will to make tough choices and lead the nation to the shared sacrifices necessary to restore some semblance of stability. But the states are the foundation of our federal union, and so they can provide guidance and examples of the kind of governance that can make the pursuit of happiness a race more people might actually win.

Wisconsin, a longtime Democratic stronghold, elected a Republican governor, Scott Walker, and Republican U.S. senator,

Ron Johnson, in 2010. Not that the Badger State has suddenly become a conservative stronghold, but voters sought an alternative to the status quo, and the resulting reforms have been so successful that Walker is routinely talked about as a presidential candidate.

In deep-blue New Jersey, a Republican governor has become a star by winning converts to such unfamiliar principles as restraining union thuggery and out-of-control spending. Chris Christie may be a figure of some controversy among Republicans, but there is no doubting that he has changed the conversation. That's what any conservative must do in order to extract ourselves from the quicksand of statism. That's exactly what Ronald Reagan did. He assumed the leadership of a country that was economically crippled and whose military power was deteriorating, and through the skillful communication of powerful ideas to the American people, he enjoyed two landslide electoral victories.

Reagan did not win by moving toward the center; he attracted the center toward himself. He made his sensible ideas appealing to people and persuaded them to broaden their thinking beyond entrenched habits of mind, wrongheaded notions that were contributing to American decline. Texans can do that too. Our success will provoke curiosity and eventually appreciation of the policies that produced it.

Sounds like a plateful of platitudes, but those things are the fuel of Texas success: solid conservative principles and a tough and self-reliant mindset that has made it possible for us to create a booming economy in the midst of recession, even as others scoff, and to offer a beacon of hope to those in the rest of the country who are not ready to concede the inevitability of American decline.

Call it Texas exceptionalism. Shouldn't every state feel the same way? The Texas version says, "We're just better, and we're going to show you why." This attitude drives some people crazy and spurs them to accuse Texans of having some kind of superiority complex.

Guilty as charged.

That doesn't mean we think less of others—or that we think every state can't achieve what we have. Again, it's not a zero-sum game. Nothing would please us more than for our fellow Americans in New York, Illinois, and even California to kick their addictions to unions and paternalistic governance and to challenge us on the economic battlefield. Let them fight us for the best economic climate. Let them contest us for every new business and every entrepreneur. The mind reels imagining the national prosperity that could result.

And the ensuing benefits would not be merely economic. Success from limited government and free-market reform in a few states could educate millions of voters on the wisdom of seeking national candidates with the same tastes. We could see a Texas-inspired true American renaissance.

* * *

So is Texas America's last, best hope? We don't want to think of ourselves as nearing some terrible brink, but it might not take many more election cycles for America finally to surrender its place in the world as a beacon of liberty, strength, and prosperity. But if it's unclear whether we're in "last hope" territory, I think Texas is definitely the "best hope." Ideas from Texas can take root anywhere and help everywhere. It is a vast task needing every platform and all the communication skills we evangelists for Lone

Star success can muster, but it has to start somewhere, and if not now, when?

Two terms of Obama, aided by his congressional co-conspirators, have been enough to send many Americans in search of alternatives in 2014 and 2016. Fifty years ago, Texans embraced Lyndon Johnson and his fatally flawed plan for a "Great Society." It took a while, but we got smarter. Since the mid-nineties, Texans have bucked the national trend by taxing less, spending less, and regulating less. It works! Any set of honest, open eyes can see it.

We're talking about *American* ideas; no state needs to become a clone of Texas. Ohio will be Ohio, Missouri will be Missouri, and you can bet New York and California will maintain their bold personalities.

But surely Californians must look back wistfully at the era when Americans were singing "California, here I come!" Now they come to my state. That growth has been a blessing, but there are plenty of Texans who would love to see some other states become similar magnets. Some Texas communities build a new high school every couple of years and seem to sprout a new restaurant every day around noon. As soon as we widen our roads, they're too narrow to accommodate the new Texans who arrived during the construction. So we don't merely welcome the idea of shared good fortune, we actively root for it. Please, other states, take some of these people. We will all do fine. (I am only partially kidding.)

And when a wave of states inspired and enlightened by Texas recover their fiscal and social health by following our example, we won't demand credit. We'll be there cheering on every state whose citizens achieve the clarity that allowed us to get our act together. We haven't cornered the market on good ideas. We just had the nerve and the attitude to enact them.

ACKNOWLEDGMENTS

My professional life involves eight-hundred-word bursts of writing and three-hour chunks of talk shows. This whole book thing is very new. It involved discipline I did not have, and probably still don't. But I hope it all works out, and for the chance to test those waters, I am grateful to a publishing house that has already done much for me.

I've been reading Regnery books for years, often in preparation for welcoming the author to the radio, but usually because I admired the writer or found the subject interesting and important. To be one of those authors offering up a subject I hope will similarly attract others is quite a wonderful twist, and I appreciate it deeply.

The dedication page is for my wife and kids, but they get an extra mention here because I hope they appreciate how much this work, and all I do, is for them. I hope Lisa knows how much I appreciate the love and support she gave me while I wrote. Just a look or a smile from her was enough to power me through some hectic days. I hope Regina will see what her dad has done and be inspired by it. I hope Ethan will know how much I appreciate the times I had to delay driveway basketball to crank out another chapter, and that I noticed the inch he grew while I was at the keyboard.

I am blessed with daily work that puts me in a radio studio with people who are a joy to create with. Executive Producers Susan Cloud and Ronda Kay Moreland, Technical Director Shane Bell, and News Director Gordon Griffin are not just coworkers I appreciate but friends I value more every day.

That work environment is made possible by Salem Communications, who plucked me from one of those radio industry rough patches in 2012 and allowed me to stay in a place I love, doing what I love. For that, I love them too, from top management in Camarillo, California, to the New York programming leadership of Phil Boyce, to my Texas managers to whom I owe so much: John Peroyea, who oversees my local radio exploits, and Greg Anderson and Tom Tradup, who plug me into the Salem Radio Network Fridays on Bill Bennett's *Morning in America*.

The *Dallas Morning News* has run my column for almost a decade. Over that same time period, the Dallas–Fort Worth Fox affiliate, KDFW, and the ABC affiliate, WFAA, have welcomed me as a regular contributor, allowing me to spout off on issues of the day. Their hospitality has allowed me to cobble together a multimedia reputation, and I am proud to work with them.

This means I have gathered readers and viewers in addition to listeners. To anyone reading this because you have seen a column I wrote, listened to a show I hosted, or watched me on a TV segment, thanks for taking the leap with me into this format. I am humbled and honored to be part of your life.

I wouldn't be who I am or where I am without my parents, Stan and Eleanor Davis, who both passed away in 1998. They gave me forty years of uninterrupted love, starting with a childhood as happy as I could ever want. I thank Mom for the gift of the love of language, and I thank Dad for his example of devotion to country and devotion to a son. In the years since, Lisa's wonderful parents, Jimmy and Shirlee Lee, have become my father and mother, and I am proud to be their son.

In closing with my thanks to God, I want to share some views on thanking God. I have seen everyone thank Him, from country music award winners to athletes who just caught the winning touchdown. I was once a little jaded about that, wondering if people thanked Him so publicly just to make themselves look good.

I am over that silliness. I can't read minds. I don't know who is sincere and who is posturing. But what difference does it make? Time spent thanking God is time well spent, and after what He has done for me, my gratitude to Him goes beyond this book to every other blessing in my life—the family, friends, and work I mentioned above, the house I live in, the blessings large and small that I do not deserve.

And finally, thank *you*. If you have never been to Texas, come see what I'm talking about. You will not find the skyline of Manhattan, the beaches of California, or the mountains of Colorado. But you'll find shining cities filled with businesses prospering in a state that's glad to have them. You'll even find Texas beaches and Texas mountains, which we're proud of because ... well, if it's part of our state, we're proud of it.

And you will find Texans. Some by birth, some by recent arrival. Don't be surprised if you feel the urge to become one. Come on in, we'll make room.

NOTES

INTRODUCTION

1.   Gallup, "Satisfaction with the United States," accessed February 2014, http://www.gallup.com/poll/1669/general-mood-country.aspx; and BOR PAC, "BOR Poll: Texans Deeply Divided on Rick Perry, Direction of Texas, Issues Facing State," Burnt Orange Report, April 11, 2012, http://www.burntorangereport.com/diary/12128/bor-poll-texans-deeply-divided-on-rick-perry-direction-of-texas-issues-facing-state.

CHAPTER TWO: WHY EVERYONE SHOULD REMEMBER THE ALAMO

1.   Alberto Riva, "What If Texas Really Were Its Own Country?," *International Business Times*, November 14, 2012, http://www.ibtimes.com/what-if-texas-really-were-its-own-country-880112.

CHAPTER THREE: THE TEXAS ECONOMY: MIRACLE OR MYTH?

1.   Paul Krugman, "The Texas Unmiracle," *New York Times*, August 24, 2011, http://www.nytimes.com/2011/08/15/opinion/the-texas-unmiracle.html?_r=0.

2. See data in the Local Area Unemployment Statistics, Bureau of Labor Statistics, http://www.bls.gov/lau/.

3. Kevin Williamson, "Paul Krugman Is Still Wrong About Texas," National Review Online, August 15, 2011, http://www.nationalreview.com/exchequer/274695/paul-krugman-still-wrong-about-texas.

CHAPTER FOUR: BAILOUT-FREE ZONE: THE VALUE OF FAILURE

1. David Streitfeld and Gretchen Morgenson, "Building Flawed American Dreams," New York Times, October 8, 2008, http://www.nytimes.com/2008/10/19/business/19cisneros.html?pagewanted=all.

CHAPTER FIVE: A STORM SHELTER FROM THE RECESSION

1. Tyler Cowen, "Why Texas Is Our Future," Time, October 28, 2013.

2. Chuck DeVore, "Texas v. California: The Real Facts behind the Lone Star State's Miracle," Forbes, July 3, 2013, http://www.forbes.com/sites/realspin/2013/07/03/texas-v-california-the-real-facts-behind-the-lone-star-states-miracle/.

3. "WSJ Lauds Texas Economy, Marked by Lots of Jobs (Including a Lot of Low-Paying Ones)," Washington Independent, June 15, 2011, http://washingtonindependent.com/110054/wsj-lauds-texas-economy-marked-by-jobs-including-a-lot-of-low-paying-ones.

CHAPTER SIX: TEXAS TAXES, PART ONE: INDIVIDUALS

1. Robert Higgs, "Kasich Takes Steps on Pledge to Phase Out Income Tax: PolitiFact Ohio," Cleveland Plain Dealer, February 12, 2013, http://www.cleveland.com/open/index.ssf/2013/02/kasich_takes_steps_on_pledge_t.html.

2. Ted Cruz, "Politifact Got It Wrong: Dewhurst's Wage Tax Was Really an Income Tax," Austin American-Statesman, February 24, 2012, http://www.statesman.com/news/news/opinion/cruz-politifact-got-it-wrong-dewhursts-wage-tax-wa/nRkjk/.

3. Joshua Blank and Jim Henson, "The Morning After for Texas Democrats," Texas Tribune, July 12, 2013, http://www.texastribune.org/2013/07/12/morning-after-texas-democrats/.

4. Brandon Formby, "Two Texas House Races in Dallas County Raise Specter of Income Tax," Dallas Morning News, October 21, 2010, http://www.dallasnews.com/news/community-news/coppell/headlines/20101021-2-Texas-House-races-in-Dallas-430.ece#.

5. The Tax Foundation, state tax climate pages, all accessed February 2014: California, http://taxfoundation.org/state-tax-climate/california; Texas, http://taxfoundation.org/state-tax-climate/texas; New York, http://taxfoundation.org/state-tax-climate/new-york.

CHAPTER SEVEN: TEXAS TAXES, PART TWO: BUSINESSES

1. Mark J. Perry, "The U-Haul Index," *AEIdeas* (blog), American Enterprise Institute, September 29, 2009, http://www.aei-ideas.org/2009/09/the-u-haul-index/.
2. Philip Rucker, "Mitt Romney Says 'Corporations Are People' at Iowa State Fair," *Washington Post*, August 11, 2011, http://articles.washingtonpost.com/2011-08-11/politics/35270239_1_romney-supporters-mitt-romney-private-sector-experience.
3. Aman Batheja, "Is Texas Really a Leader in Low Taxes?," *Fort Worth Star-Telegram*, September 25, 2011, http://www.star-telegram.com/2011/09/25/3395762/is-texas-really-a-leader-in-low.html.
4. Texas Wide Open for Business, Texas Economic Development Division, Office of the Governor, http://www.texaswideopenforbusiness.com/incentives-financing/tax/index.php.
5. Sam Wyly and Andrew Wyly, *Texas Got it Right!* (New York: Melcher Media, 2012), 100.

CHAPTER EIGHT: A PARTNER, NOT A PUNISHER: REGULATION AND COMMON SENSE

1. Peggy Venable, "President Obama's Rule Review: Start with the EPA," Americans for Prosperity, Texas, January 18, 2011, http://americansforprosperity.org/texas/legislativealerts/011811-president-obamas-rule-review-start-epa/.
2. Emily Stephenson, "States, Texas Bank File Appeal in Dodd-Frank Law Challenge," Reuters, August 2, 2012, http://www.reuters.com/article/2013/08/02/us-usa-court-texasbank-idUSBRE97117A20130802.
3. John Daniel Davidson, "Helping Hands Off," *Texas Monthly*, August 2013, http://www.texasmonthly.com/story/helping-hands.

CHAPTER NINE: TORT REFORM: A MAGNET FOR BUSINESSES

1. American Tort Reform Association, *Bringing Justice to Judicial Hellholes, 2002*, judicialhellholes.org, http://www.judicialhellholes.org/wp-content/uploads/2010/12/JH2002.pdf.

2. Joseph Nixon and Texas Public Policy Foundation, "Ten Years of Tort Reform in Texas: A Review," Backgrounder 2830, Heritage Foundation, July 26, 2013, http://www.heritage.org/research/reports/2013/07/ten-years-of-tort-reform-in-texas-a-review#_ftn1.

3. Ibid.

4. "Ten-Gallon Tort Reform," *Wall Street Journal*, June 6, 2003, http://online.wsj.com/news/articles/SB105485752433018000.

5. Associated Press, Ten Years of Tort Reform in Texas Bring Fewer Suits, Lower Payouts," Insurance Journal, September 3, 2013, http://www.insurancejournal.com/news/southcentral/2013/09/03/303718.htm.

6. *A Texas Turnaround: The Impact of Lawsuit Reform on Business Activity in the Lone Star State*, The Perryman Group, http://tlrfoundation.com/beta/files/Texas_Tort_Reform_Report_2008.pdf.

7. Nixon and the Texas Public Policy Foundation, "Ten Years of Tort Reform in Texas."

CHAPTER TEN: COWBOYS, CATTLE, AND COTTON: TEXAS BEFORE OIL

1. U.S. Fish and Wildlife Service, "Time Line of the American Bison," http://www.fws.gov/bisonrange/timeline.htm.

2. Randolph B. Campbell, *Gone to Texas: A History of the Lone Star State* (New York: Oxford University Press, 2003), 297.

3. Texas Historical Commission, "The Chisholm Trail: Exploring the Folklore and Legacy," http://www.thc.state.tx.us/public/upload/publications/chisholm-trail.pdf.

4. Texas State Historical Association, "Lumber Industry," http://www.tshaonline.org/handbook/online/articles/drl02.

CHAPTER ELEVEN: FROM SPINDLETOP TO THE SPACE AGE

1. Robert Wooster and Christine Moor Sanders, "Spindletop Oilfield," *Handbook of Texas Online*, Texas State Historical Association, https://www.tshaonline.org/handbook/online/articles/dos03.

2. Ben H. Procter, "Great Depression," *Handbook of Texas Online*, https://www.tshaonline.org/handbook/online/articles/npg01.

CHAPTER TWELVE: COOKING WITH GAS

1. U.S. Energy Information Administration, "Energy Flow, 2011," *Annual Energy Review, 2011*, accessed February 2014, http://www.eia.gov/totalenergy/data/annual/pdf/sec1_3.pdf.

2. U.S. Energy Information Administration, "Coal," accessed February 2014, http://www.eia.gov/coal/.

3. U.S. Energy Information Administration, "Rankings: Natural Gas Marketed Production, 2011," accessed February 2014, http://www.eia.gov/state/rankings/?sid=US#/series/47.

CHAPTER THIRTEEN: A LOOSER LASSO: THE PATH TO PRODUCTIVITY

1. "Railroad Commission of Texas," Texas State Library Commission, Texas Archival Resources Online, http://www.lib.utexas.edu/taro/tslac/10226/tsl-10226.html.

2. Beth Cortez-Neavel, "Anti-Federal Sentiment Dominates Discussion of Texas Oil and Gas Industry," *Texas Observer*, January 10, 2013, http://www.texasobserver.org/anti-federal-sentiment-dominates-discussion-of-texas-oil-and-gas-industr/.

3. David Blackmon, "The Texas Shale Oil and Gas Revolution—Leading the Way to Enhanced Energy Security," *Forbes*, March 19, 2013, http://www.forbes.com/sites/davidblackmon/2013/03/19/the-texas-shale-oil-gas-revolution-leading-the-way-to-enhanced-energy-security/.

4. Chuck DeVore, *The Texas Model: Prosperity in the Lone Star State and Lessons for America* (CreateSpace Publishing Platform, 2013), 92.

5. Reuters, "Texas Electric Grid Sets New Wind Generation Record," February 13, 2012, http://www.reuters.com/article/2013/02/14/utilities-texas-wind-idUSL1N0BE04N20130214.

6. Sam Wyly and Andrew Wyly, *Texas Got It Right!* (New York: Melcher Media, 2012), 92.

7. Herman K. Trabish, "Ten Years of Texas Electric Utility Deregulation," Greentech Media, January 24, 2012, http://www.greentechmedia.com/articles/read/Ten-Years-in-Texas-Electric-Utility-Deregulation.

8. Nicholas Sakelaris, "JD Power Ranks Texas' Electric Providers," *Dallas Business Journal*, August 15, 2013, http://www.bizjournals.com/dallas/news/2013/08/14/jd-power-ranks-texas-electric-providers.html?page=all.

9. Environmental Protection Agency, "Houston Air Quality Continues to Improve; Ozone Pollution Declines despite Population Growth," news

release, August 28, 2013, http://yosemite.epa.gov/opa/admpress.nsf/0/
B64F2486F17C53FE85257BD500704F85.

10.   James Ragland, "American Lung Association Gives Dallas County 'F'
       Grade for Its Ozone Level but Says Air Quality Is Improving," *Dallas
       Morning News*, April 24, 2013, http://thescoopblog.dallasnews.
       com/2013/04/american-lung-association-gives-dallas-county-f-grade-
       for-its-ozone-level-but-says-air-quality-is-improving.html/.

CHAPTER FOURTEEN: ILLEGAL AND LEGAL, PROTEST AND PROGRESS

1.   "How Mass (Legal) Immigration Dooms a Conservative Republican
       Party," Eagle Forum, http://www.eagleforum.org/immigration.html.

2.   Pei Li, "Illegal Immigration Shifts to Texas as Overall Numbers Fall on
       Border," *Arizona Capitol Times*, September 30, 2013, http://
       azcapitoltimes.com/news/2013/09/30/illegal-immigration-shifts-to-
       texas-as-overall-numbers-fall-on-border/.

3.   "The American Opportunity: Making Immigration Work," U.S.
       Chamber of Commerce immigration issues page, http://immigration.
       uschamber.com.

CHAPTER SIXTEEN: OUR HISPANIC FUTURE

1.   Zac Crain, "Is Jason Villalba the Future of the Texas GOP?" *D Magazine*,
       October 2012, http://www.dmagazine.com/publications/d-magazine
       /2012/october/is-jason-villalba-the-future-of-the-texas-gop.

2.   Author interview with Jason Villalba, December 4, 2013.

3.   Andrew Dugan, "Texas Hispanics Tilt Democratic, but State Likely to
       Stay Red," Gallup Politics, February 7, 2014, http://www.gallup.com/
       poll/167339/texan-hispanics-tilt-democratic-state-likely-stay-red.aspx.

CHAPTER SEVENTEEN: THE TEXAS TAPESTRY

1.   Ryan Robinson, "Top Ten Demographic Trends in Austin," http://
       austintexas.gov/page/top-ten-demographic-trends-austin-texas.

CHAPTER EIGHTEEN: LIVING WHERE WE PLEASE

1.   An excerpt from Mr. Kurtz's book was published as "How Obama is
       Robbing the Suburbs to Pay for the Cities," *Forbes*, August 13, 2012,
       http://www.forbes.com/sites/realspin/2012/08/13/how-obama-is-
       robbing-the-suburbs-to-pay-for-the-cities/.

CHAPTER NINETEEN: EDUCATION: HOW TO FUND, WHAT TO TEACH?

1. Erica Grieder, *Big, Hot, Cheap, and Right: What America Can Learn from the Strange Genius of Texas* (New York: Public Affairs, 2013), 64.

2. Deroy Murdock, "Education Spending Soars, Test Scores Stagnate," *Corner* (blog), National Review Online, August 7, 2013, http://www.nationalreview.com/corner/355271/education-spending-soars-test-scores-stagnate-deroy-murdock.

3. Ryan Holeywell, "Education Spending per Student per State," *Governing*, accessed February 2014, http://www.governing.com/gov-data/education-data/state-education-spending-per-pupil-data.html.

4. Terrence Stutz, "Texas High School Graduation Rate Improves," *Dallas Morning News*, August 6, 2013, http://educationblog.dallasnews.com/2013/08/texas-high-school-graduation-rate-improves.html/.

5. New York State Education Department, "Statewide High School Graduation Rate Stays at 74% despite Higher Graduation Standards," press release, June 17, 2013, http://www.tea.state.tx.us/index4.aspx?id=25769806896.

6. Texas Education Agency, "Texas ACT Scores for Various Groups Hit New Highs," press release, August 21, 2013, http://www.tea.state.tx.us/index4.aspx?id=25769806896.

7. Laura Heinauer, "State Science Curriculum Director Resigns," *Austin American-Statesman*, November 29, 2007, http://web.archive.org/web/20071201151343/http://www.statesman.com/news/content/news/stories/local/11/29/1129science.html.

CHAPTER TWENTY: UNION-PROOF: THE RIGHTNESS OF RIGHT-TO-WORK

1. James Hohman and Jarrett Skorup, "Fact and Fiction about Right-to-Work: A Reality Check at the One-Year Anniversary," Michigan Capitol Confidential, Mackinac Center for Public Policy, December 10, 2013, https://www.mackinac.org/19429.

CHAPTER TWENTY-ONE: CHOOSING LIFE IN THE HOME OF *ROE V. WADE*

1. Emily Swanson and Mark Blumenthal, "Abortion Poll Finds Support for 20-Week Ban," Huffington Post, July 11, 2013, http://www.huffingtonpost.com/2013/07/11/abortion-poll_n_3575551.html.

2. Guttmacher Institute, "State Facts about Abortion: Texas," accessed February 2014, http://www.guttmacher.org/pubs/sfaa/texas.html.

CHAPTER TWENTY-TWO: STICKING TO OUR GUNS

1. Drew DeSilver, "A Minority of Americans Own Guns, but Just How Many Is Unclear," Pew Research Center, June 4, 2013, http://www.pewresearch.org/fact-tank/2013/06/04/a-minority-of-americans-own-guns-but-just-how-many-is-unclear/.

2. Ross Ramsey, "UT/TT Poll: Texans (Mostly) Don't Want More Gun Laws," *Texas Tribune*, March 5, 2013, http://www.texastribune.org/2013/03/05/uttt-poll-texans-mostly-dont-want-more-gun-laws/.

3. Robert Wilonsky, "In an Arlington Strip Mall, a Showdown between Open-Carry Advocates and Four Moms in a Blue Mesa," *Dallas Morning News*, November 11, 2013, http://thescoopblog.dallasnews.com/2013/11/in-an-arlington-strip-mall-a-showdown-between-open-carry-advocates-and-four-moms-in-a-blue-mesa.html/.

CHAPTER TWENTY-THREE: CRIME AND PUNISHMENT

1. Texas Department of Criminal Justice, "Executed Offenders," updated February 6, 2014, http://www.tdcj.state.tx.us/death_row/dr_executed_offenders.html.

2. Death Penalty Information Center, "Murder Rates Nationally and by State," accessed February 2014, http://www.deathpenaltyinfo.org/murder-rates-nationally-and-state#MRalpha.

3. "Texas Law Enforcement Agency Uniform Crime Reports: Texas Crime Rates, 1960–2012," DisasterCenter.com, accessed February 2014, http://www.disastercenter.com/crime/txcrime.htm.

4. Chuck DeVore, *The Texas Model: Prosperity in the Lone Star State and Lessons for America* (Austin: Texas Public Policy Foundation, 2012) 122–23.

5. Editorial Board, "Texas's Progress on Juvenile Justice," *New York Times*, July 9, 2011.

CHAPTER TWENTY-FOUR: GOD'S COUNTRY

1. Texas State Historical Association, "Religion," Texas Almanac, accessed February 2014, http://www.texasalmanac.com/topics/religion.

2. Texas State Historical Association, "Religion in Early Texas," Texas Almanac, accessed February 2014, http://www.texasalmanac.com/topics/history/religion-early-texas.

CHAPTER TWENTY-FIVE: SUPPORTING OUR TROOPS *AND* WHAT THEY DO

1. *2011 Demographics: Profile of the Military Community*, Office of the Deputy Under Secretary of Defense, updated November 2012, http://www.militaryonesource.mil/12038/MOS/Reports/2011_Demographics_Report.pdf.

CHAPTER TWENTY-SIX: CALIFORNIA: THE ANTI-TEXAS

1. Chuck DeVore, "Texas v. California: The Real Facts behind the Lone Star State's Miracle,'" *Forbes*, July 3, 2013, http://www.forbes.com/sites/realspin/2013/07/03/texas-v-california-the-real-facts-behind-the-lone-star-states-miracle/print/.
2. Tom Gray and Robert Scardamalia, *The Great California Exodus: A Closer Look*, Civic Report no. 71, Center for State and Local Leadership (New York: Manhattan Institute for Policy Research, September 2012), https://www.manhattan-institute.org/html/cr_71.htm#.UrMyjZFWJbo.

CHAPTER TWENTY-SEVEN: TARGETING TEXAS

1. Jesse McKinley, "Comment by Cuomo Outrages Republicans," January 22, 2014, http://www.nytimes.com/2014/01/23/nyregion/cuomo-comment-elicits-retort-from-republicans.html?_r=0.
2. Casey Seller, "Cuomo: 'Extreme Conservatives … Have No Place in the State of New York,'" *Albany Times-Union*, January 17, 2014, http://blog.timesunion.com/capitol/archives/203801/cuomo-extreme-conservatives-have-no-place-in-the-state-of-new-york/.
3. Brian Domitrovic, "Big-Government Stirrings in Texas, the Most Important Place in the World," *Forbes*, January 21, 2014, http://www.forbes.com/sites/briandomitrovic/2014/01/21/big-government-stirrings-in-texas-the-most-important-place-in-the-world/.

CHAPTER TWENTY-EIGHT: NORTH DAKOTA

1. Steve Hargreaves, "North Dakota Grows Five Times Faster Than Nation," CNN, June 6, 2013, http://money.cnn.com/2013/06/06/news/economy/north-dakota-economy/.
2. Curt Brown, "A Year in North Dakota: Stories of People and Change," *Minneapolis Star Tribune*, January 6, 2014, http://www.startribune.com/local/238667221.html.

3.　　Brian Naylor, "Pro-Oil Democrat in the Hunt For N.D. Senate Seat," NPR, October 15, 2012, http://www.npr.org/2012/10/15/162954683/pro-oil-democrat-in-the-hunt-for-n-d-senate-seat.

CHAPTER TWENTY-NINE: PENNSYLVANIA

1.　　Timothy Puko, "Pennsylvania Vies for Being No. 2 U.S. Gas Producer," *Pittsburgh Tribune-Review*, August 16, 2013, http://triblive.com/state/pennsylvania/4545504-74/gas-state-natural#axzz2cR6vuSiB.

2.　　Stephen Fehr and Melissa Maynard, "North Dakota's Oil and Tax Windfall Now $1.3B," *Fiscal Times*, August 28, 2013, http://www.thefiscaltimes.com/Articles/2013/08/28/North-Dakotas-Oil-and-Tax-Windfall-Now-1-3B.

3.　　Talia Buford, "Natural Gas Lights Up the Race for Pennsylvania Governor," Politico, November 12, 2013, http://www.politico.com/story/2013/11/natural-gas-energy-pennsylvania-governor-race-2014-election-tom-corbett-allyson-schwartz-99678.html.

4.　　Ken Silverstein,"Pennsylvania and New York Are a Thousand Miles Apart on Shale Gas Fracking," EnergyBiz.com, August 19, 2013, http://www.energybiz.com/article/13/08/pennsylvania-and-new-york-are-thousand-miles-apart-shale-gas-fracking.

5.　　Mario Cattabiani and Amy Worden, "How Marcellus Shale Gas Came to Be Tax-Exempt in Pa.," *Philadelphia Inquirer*, October 25, 2009, http://www.philly.com/philly/news/special_packages/inquirer/marcellus-shale/20091025_How_Marcellus_Shale_gas_came_to_be_tax-exempt_in_Pa_.html.

CHAPTER THIRTY: INDIANA

1.　　David Leonhardt, "Budget Hawk Eyes Deficit," *New York Times*, January 4, 2011, http://www.nytimes.com/2011/01/05/business/economy/05leonhardt.html?pagewanted=all&_r=1&.

2.　　Christina Captides and John Hendren, "Straw Vote: Conservatives Hand Mike Pence the Keys to the Car," ABC News, September 19, 2010, http://abcnews.go.com/Politics/values-voters-summit-pick-mike-pence-straw-poll/story?id=11672930.

3.　　"The Best States For Business and Careers," *Forbes*, September 25, 2013, http://www.forbes.com/best-states-for-business/#page:1_sort:0_direction:asc_search:.

CHAPTER THIRTY-ONE: NORTH CAROLINA

1. Michael A. Fletcher, "In North Carolina, Unimpeded GOP Drives State Hard to the Right," *Washington Post*, May 25, 2013, http://www.washingtonpost.com/business/economy/in-north-carolina-unimpeded-gop-drives-state-hard-to-the-right/2013/05/25/a9c9ccd2-c3c7-11e2-914f-a7aba60512a7_story.html.

CHAPTER THIRTY-TWO: GOVERNOR RICK PERRY

1. Andrew Rosenthal, "Rick Perry Won't Run," *Taking Note* (blog), *New York Times*, July 8, 2013, http://takingnote.blogs.nytimes.com/2013/07/08/rick-perry-wont-run-for-governor/.

2. Liz Austin Peterson, "Texas Gov. Orders Anti-Cancer Vaccine," *Washington Post*, February 3, 2007, http://www.washingtonpost.com/wp-dyn/content/article/2007/02/03/AR2007020300276.html.

3. Ibid.

CHAPTER THIRTY-THREE: SENATOR TED CRUZ

1. Rasmussen Reports, "23% Name Pope Francis Most Influential, 21% Say Obama," December 15, 2013, http://www.rasmussenreports.com/public_content/lifestyle/people/december_2013/23_name_pope_francis_most_influential_21_say_obama.

CHAPTER THIRTY-FIVE: OUR LAST, BEST HOPE?

1. Paul Gleiser, "You Tell Me," KTBB, December 19, 2013, http://www.ktbb.com/youtellme/2013/12/19/boomers-to-grads-sorry-but-we-spent-all-the-money/.

INDEX